Carters Book for the Casual Gardener

Also published by Heinemann:

CARTERS BOOK FOR GARDENERS
A. G. L. Hellyer

CARTERS DICTIONARY OF GARDENING
Compiled by Oliver Dawson

Carters Book for the Casual Gardener

Jim Mather

Gardening Editor, the Sunday Mirror

in collaboration with
CARTERS TESTED SEEDS LTD

HEINEMANN : LONDON

William Heinemann Ltd
15 Queen St, Mayfair, London W1X 8BE

LONDON MELBOURNE TORONTO
JOHANNESBURG AUCKLAND

First published 1975
434 91237 9

Printed in Great Britain by
Jarrold & Sons Ltd, Norwich

Contents

Foreword

We have felt for some time that there was an empty space on gardening bookshelves. The keen gardener and the specialist plantsmen were well catered for, but the casual gardener seemed to be more or less ignored.

This book has been written especially for the new gardener and for the busy householder who has little time and perhaps less inclination to 'do' the garden. It takes into account the time-consuming needs of modern living and recognizes that there are other pastimes that attract the garden-owner. It is in itself a short-cut to gardening and removes much of the toil and mystique that are relics of a bygone age.

Jim Mather, who wrote the book for us, is himself a very busy man who combines writing on gardening in *The Sunday Mirror* and other publications with tending a very large garden in Surrey. He found that in his own garden he had to equate little time with large space and, therefore, he writes with complete authority.

We commend this book to all who feel that their gardens get the better of them and to those who want a good show of colour and plenty of fresh vegetables for the least amount of effort.

CARTERS TESTED SEEDS LTD

Upper Dee Mills,
Llangollen,
Clwyd.

Carters Seeds Ltd. and Samuel Dobie & Son Ltd., Llangollen, supplied most of the illustrations in the book. Mr. Ernest L. Crowson did a series of photographs in the author's garden. The author is extremely grateful also for the loan of pictures from Andrews of Hindhead, Birmid Qualcast, Flymo, Imperial Chemical Industries, T. Parker & Sons (Turf Management), H. C. W. Shaw (Floracolour), Stephen Treseder & Son, and John Waterer Sons & Crisp.

1 Objective

Everyone loves a garden but not everyone loves gardening. There is no reason why people should not be able to enjoy their likes without getting an overdose of their pet dislikes. Even if you like gardening, it need not take up time you may have to spend elsewhere and on other things. Given the right ideas and the right tools, we can take our gardening casually, and sometimes lazily, whether we want to put in two hours a day or just two hours a week on it.

This book is to help all who think on those lines. It is a guide for all beginners; for those who don't know where to start; for those who have no time to spare; for the lazy man who wants to keep up with the neighbours. A friend suggested the sub-title 'For the idle and the ignorant', but you would not be reading it if you were idle or ignorant. A better sub-title would be: 'For busy, intelligent people'. I suppose we all have a streak of laziness in us, and why not? It may spur us to apply skill instead of brawn.

Gardening is for leisure and pleasure. People who make hard work of it are probably victims of an attitude of mind; a misguided or subconscious striving after top professional standards.

The lawn does not have to compete with the Test Match wicket at Lord's, or the Centre Court at Wimbledon. That sort of groundsmanship demands a great deal of time and skill. Even an immaculate garden lawn does not need such skill, and it is easy to maintain a pleasant patch of green if equipment and method are right. You can have an easy garden, which is a joy to look at, providing you adopt the

A happy marriage between stone, grass, and flowers

right approach. The Saturday afternoon golfer has no thought of playing up to international or professional standards. He soon recognizes his rating, and is content to play to that or to try to improve his handicap by eliminating obvious faults – but not by making hard work of it. This is an attitude which the busy man might adopt towards his gardening. It is not a matter of accepting poor standards but of seeking to get maximum effect in return for minimum effort.

If your kitchen was old-fashioned and full of tiresome chores you might decide to make it labour-saving. Would you achieve it by sitting back and letting the dishes pile up in the sink? More likely you would begin by doing extra work: replanning and re-equipping; planning a compact layout and installing labour-saving equipment such as a washing-machine, a cooker with automatic settings, and gadgets for speeding routine tasks. The garden, like the kitchen, is part of the home; and gardening, like cooking and its attendant chores, is part of life. Life is for living, and if we are to enjoy it we must enjoy all of it, including the housework, cooking, and gardening. By making tasks pleasant and cutting down the time spent on them, we make time to extend our activities, and thus enrich our lives. Of course, some of us truly enjoy gardening, just as I know some people enjoy cooking. But no matter how much fun and satisfaction we get out of our activities, we have a duty to seek the best, quickest, or most leisurely way of pursuing them.

The science of Work Study aims at finding easy, efficient, and speedy ways of doing a job. It seeks first to decide whether the job can be eliminated, so that the worker can switch his time to something more productive. When we do a gardening chore, we should ask ourselves 'Is it necessary?' Do we need that sharp neat edge to the lawn? There are ways of avoiding it, such as letting the lawn run right into the hedge bottom. Even if we keep that neat straight lawn edge, we can make the job easier and quicker by using a powered machine.

In planning, we have to think of the people who use the garden, as well as the plot itself. It would be sad to remove a tree because it is giving too much shade, and then find that there is no longer a shady spot to sit in. You might want a garden machine powered by mains electricity. It can be disappointing if your layout makes it impossible to trail an electric cable across the garden without damage to plants in the way. Does your plan leave room for such pleasures as having tea on the lawn? Is there a place where the garden tent can stand clear of the prevailing wind? Have the children room to play safely? Is there a place to hang the washing? These questions should caution you against rushing to make changes before you read the book.

You may ask why this casual gardening is not taught in all gardening manuals. It *is* taught, though perhaps not with much emphasis. The gardening manual teaches how to get the *best* results. Most people accept this counsel of perfection as if it were the only possible way. Do not blame the writers, for they assume you will want the highest standards. The aim of this book is to shift the emphasis on to easy ways of maintaining the garden. This may not help you to carry off show prizes but it will show how you can still have a lovely garden. The ultimate answer must strike a balance between the desirable but difficult, and the leisurely but attainable. The making of the easy garden must involve a certain amount of work, such as perhaps the removal of a time-consuming feature and the installation of one which needs no labour. Some of this rebuilding can be done with little effort but some may involve work. You have to face up to the job of putting the garden into the desired shape, before you can sit back and enjoy the extra time

Paving stones and a profusion of flowers leave no room for weeds

won by bringing in work-saving ideas and cutting out tiresome features.

Occasionally – only rarely, I am happy to say – I come across a small front garden that has been covered over with concrete to cut out cultivation. It looks ugly. If you really want to smother the soil completely and cut out cultivations you can do it in a better way. You must first work out a neat design of pathways for which you can use concrete or paving stones. Then smother the rest of the ground in a 4-inch (10 cm) layer of pleasant-coloured pebbles, and introduce just two or three plants, either in tubs or planted in the soil under the pebbles. If you use tubs they will need watering. Whatever way you do it, you will have to apply a weedkiller at least once a year, because the odd weed *will* still get up through your layer of pebbles. Some would come up even in the roadway if you stopped all traffic for a few months. But the idea described is a way of doing what was in the mind of the silly fellow who tried to hide his garden under concrete to avoid mowing and weeding.

Parts of this book will go into details on some jobs which the busy man does not want to do. Knowledge of the accepted routine helps those who want to take short-cuts. It is the wise man rather than the uninformed who knows best how to take evasive action. Part of the art of avoiding major problems is to recognize them while they are still minor ones. You may prefer never to look under the bonnet of your car, but knowing what goes on under the bonnet helps you recognize the signs which tell you when to call in a mechanic. Some of the work of creating an easy garden can be done for you by paid labour. But knowing what is involved enables you to see that you get it done the way you want it.

2 Guidelines

The basic needs for a garden which will be easy to run are the right pattern, with the right equipment, and the right plants. These three must fit one another. Perhaps it will help us remember if we use a mnemonic – a word made up of the initial letters of the three. Pattern, Equipment, and Plants give us the mnemonic 'PEP'. Let PEP be a reminder of the factors to be borne in mind throughout your planning.

The pattern for easy gardening requires a simple and flexible layout which permits our doing as much or as little as we wish and which is not difficult to vary if we find we have forgotten some point. There must be no awkward feature interrupting the movement of essential tools and machines (who wants to carry a mower up and down steps?). We must think of rest and recreation: we don't want to struggle with deck-chairs along too-narrow paths, or manœuvre them round tight corners. Nor do we want to find that the only place for a garden chair is in full sun or permanent shade, or overlooked from all sides.

If children are to play in the back garden, they must be able to do so without danger to themselves and without undue risk of damage to property. Equipment should match the pattern and the plantings. For instance, the larger the lawn, the larger should be the mower; and the easy movement of it from its storage place to the lawn must be provided for in the garden layout. Petrol machines indicate the need for a safe spot in which to keep a small can of that terribly inflammable fuel. They call also for a small area of concrete on which to refuel and start up the engine. Doing these things on the lawn means a risk of damage to the grass due to spillage. When you start up the engine of a petrol machine on a convenient slab of concrete, you need a simple straight access from there to the point of use. Electrical equipment, such as mowers or hedge-trimmers, operated by cable from the mains, demands a layout which will allow the cable to run straight and free from tricky obstacles. The water-point is more important than many people realize. A stand-pipe properly sited in the garage or outdoors makes the chore of running out a hosepipe much slicker than the struggle to feed the hose through the kitchen window to the tap over the sink. A stand-pipe is needed also when mixing plant sprays – you don't want to mix them in the kitchen.

The whole garden concept must take into consideration what equipment will be needed, where it will be needed, and how it will be got there. Even carrying a bucket of spray liquid can be awkward if you have to get through a narrow gap in a hedge or other screen. The gap should be wider than you-plus-bucket. You should be able to carry the bucket effortlessly at your side without risk of bumping and consequent spilling of chemical mixtures. You need extra width of path or gap when carrying a hover-type lawn-mower (Flymo) because, having no wheels, it has to be carried. You can get a nasty crick in the shoulder if you try to manœuvre that sort of machine clumsily, though it is easy where space allows freedom of movement. Examples like this emphasize that the garden pattern, layout, and planting should be kept in mind when choosing equipment, and that equipment should be kept in mind when planning the layout. A pram is not garden equipment, but if there is a baby in the house the pram should be able to reach an airy, shady spot. It does not want to be near a garden pond, where there may be flies, nor should anyone need to wheel it over soft ground which will cake the wheels with mud. The pram comes into the house and on to carpeted floors, not into the garden shed, so pathways should allow it, not only easy passage, but mud-free movement.

Choice of plants is an issue on which it is wise to begin with an open mind. Some plants need absolutely *no* attention once they are planted in the right place. But if *every* plant in your garden were like that, and every space filled, your garden would be the same this year, next year, and forever – a dull prospect indeed. A cypress, a yew, a poplar, most of our woodland trees, and many of our garden trees can be planted and forgotten providing they are properly placed. But the right place is the one which will accommodate the mature tree, not just the little specimen that it was at the time you planted it. The weeping willow that looked a pleasant feature from your window as it stood gracefully in the middle of the lawn becomes a menace ten years later, when it stands like an octopus embracing and smothering the whole lawn and shutting out almost all light from the window. The stately poplar at ten years old and still growing looks a slim figure apparently taking up no width at all, but it gives you an awful shock when you find that its roots have reached right across the garden and started to lift and crack the house walls.

On the other hand, pretty subjects which you are tempted to cross off your list because they are short-lived (such as the broom) or because they need a little trimming to keep them blooming freely (such as the lilac and the forsythia) are items you might well think worth having. When you think of planting things which need absolutely no attention, be wary that there are no hidden drawbacks. And before you think of rejecting something on the ground that it may need replacing in a few years, think carefully of what you are missing. It is easy to clear out and replace a shrub which has gone scraggy because it does not age well. But it is terribly difficult and expensive to get a giant poplar removed when you find

Philadelphus Silver Showers

its roots blocking the drains or damaging the house, the water mains, and the underground cables.

Suggestions giving a wide choice of plants for all seasons and all aspects will be found in later chapters with advice on how and when to plant. Be warned against trying out gimmicky ideas which are supposed to make gardening a metaphorical bed of roses. Before adopting such notions, especially any which involve spending money on clever inventions, think twice unless someone whose word you can rely on assures you of their worth. One trap you could be tempted to fall into is the adoption of a 'no-digging' system of growing with the aim of saving yourself hard labour. This really is a nasty one, because it sounds so simple.

First of all, digging is not an operation that takes up much time in the average garden. Nor is it the hard work it is often made out to be, providing the digger adopts the right stance and knows his footwork. But more important, the technique of 'no-digging' is hard work. It involves spreading annually a layer of peat, sawdust, composted garden waste, or other material to insulate the ground, to reduce moisture loss, and smother weeds. I have known 'no-diggers' advocate spreading a 2-inch (5 cm) layer of garden compost each year on the whole cultivated area. The spadework involved in merely making the compost-heaps is enough to put off any seeker after an easy style of gardening. But loading it, barrowing it, and spreading it, add up to a fantastic amount of work. Digging is easier. The no-digging routine is a sound scientific idea, but whatever else is claimed for it, no one can seriously describe it as a way of cutting down work.

One sure way to reduce labour is to spend more money and less time over your gardening, such as by replacing your hand-propelled mower with an efficient motorized mower. But you can pour out both money and sweat in vain if you go for unsuitable items of equipment. For instance a large motorized rotary cultivator may be heavy to handle and quite incapable of proper manœuvre in a small garden, or at least it may prove harder work than using a spade in the limited area.

It is an illusion to think that you can plan a garden to fit the precise number of hours you desire to put into it. There are so many variables that the time-test can be only a guide. It can give you a clear idea of the approximate time needed for a task that gets regular attention. You can time how long it takes to hoe your border, but if the weeds are allowed to grow big and tough, and the ground is hard and dry, you may take well over the prescribed time and still not do the job satisfactorily. If the weeds are young and small and the soil is moist and crumbly, you may nip through the job in minutes and leave a perfect finish. Thus, timing can be misleading.

What is useful, however, is to time different ways of doing a job under comparable conditions to find a convincing answer to a labour-saving problem. You would probably prove, for instance, that an application of a liquid herbicide to control weeds can be made in much less time, and with less effort, than it takes to do the job with a hoe.

3 Starting at the Grass Roots

Call it virgin ground, weedy dump, or what you will, the plot of land round a newly-built house is at once a challenge and an opportunity. It challenges the occupant, but at the same time gives him a chance to impose his will more quickly than if he were taking on a ready-made garden. The new plot can vary tremendously. It may be a neat piece of meadow or a tidy area of soil giving no clue to what has been buried below the surface, or perhaps just an unattractive heap of builders' rubbish. Whatever its state, the first need is to clear it and dispose of useless debris, such as old cans. Clean debris such as tiles and brickbats should be heaped neatly in some corner, to be retrieved when needed. Or, if the line of a path or area for concreting has been decided on, it can be marked out, and this clean debris can be placed in position as foundation material. Decide whether the lie of the land is acceptable. If it slopes, you have to choose whether to leave it sloping or to terrace it; that is, to make two or three flat areas on different levels connected by steps or ramps.

Unwanted rubbish, and weeds, must be disposed of. The weeds can be cut and stacked to rot down. The other debris should either be removed from the site, or buried. If buried, it should be put deep enough to allow at least 2 feet (60 cm) of soil on top. Slice off high spots and fill up hollows. After all this clearance, we can take a long look at the plot and consider how to divide it into the three basic features: lawns, paths, and planted areas. This takes us back to the beginning, or what ought to have been the beginning if the builder had left the ground clear. Front gardens usually are small areas of decoration, whereas the back may have to provide a bit of everything, depending on what its occupant wants to make of it – lawn, plant border, food plot, space for garden shed, greenhouse, playground, and pathways – or perhaps no more than a rough lawn.

Once the ground is clear, with no sticks, stones or rubbish lying around, one can play for time in the back garden by doing nothing while making up one's mind on the PEP (pattern, equipment, and plants) mentioned earlier. Although in theory this means doing nothing, there will be growth to contend with and this growth can be rapid at some times of the year. So playing for time involves keeping down grass and weed growth while waiting. A rotary mower taken over the ground once a week will not only keep the area tidy, but will begin to produce a grass patch. How quickly this happens depends on the season, the volume of dormant seed near the soil surface, and quantities of seed blowing in from the surrounding area. In country districts bare ground simply kept mown in this way may become a grass patch in a matter of weeks. In town areas it will probably take months. But the principle is there, and it is a simple one: nature abhors a vacuum and dislikes bare ground. A square yard of ground, regardless of whether anything is growing on it, may contain up to half a million dormant seeds which can live for decades while waiting for suitable conditions to start them into growth. Those conditions are created in bringing the unseen seeds near the surface by soil disturbance, providing temperature and humidity are right.

Whether we play for time or start on our PEP right away, it is helpful to think of the area as entirely covered in grass. A plot of grass bounded by house wall and fences is hardly a garden. You can stick at that if you wish, but you are much more likely to want more, even if it is just something to break up the drab outline of the bare fence. So let us start with the pattern (the first leg of our PEP), and that means planning the garden outline. An examination of the all-grass plan shows a weakness right away. Feet may want to traverse the ground when it is winter wet and muddy. This shows the need for a pathway and its location must be decided according to its proposed uses. We are immediately confronted with other questions: shall we be having a garden shed, and if so where shall we put it? Shall we be hanging out washing and where should we hang it so that it can blow without flapping on the fence? Which way does the wind usually blow? The answer to that one will have to be taken into account in considering plantings. It is surprising how the factors interlock so that each aspect of our PEP has to be looked at in relation to the others.

We can now have a shot at a rough plan. The garden shed should go into whatever corner will best hide it, or where it will get the light you want if you are likely to work in it. The path must lead eventually to the shed whatever feature it may take in on the way. It should start at a point near the back door. Suppose the section of garden furthest from the house might some time be wanted to grow a few vegetables or some fruit. I am not wishing this on you: there is no commitment to grow anything you don't want. But a garden layout should be so planned that normal features can be introduced at any time without the need to tear the place apart and start again. So, for the strip furthest from the house, the pathway should run straight, because this would be most practical if vegetables were ever planted there. But for the first stretch of path, a curve may be desirable to allow the introduction of informal features which break up the outline and disguise the exact size of the garden. This greatly oversimplifies the art of garden design, but we are not dealing here in detail with the many landscaping features which go to make up a good design. Suffice it to say that a plan should not be symmetrical unless it is to be formal, and that nature tends to produce curves rather than straight lines. We cannot avoid the straight lines of boundary fences, but we can soften them by informality.

When the pathway is decided, the type of surfacing has to be considered. The cleanest and simplest surfacing is concrete but it is hard in outline as well as in texture. It can be improved by allowing plants to trail over its edges. Almost as efficient, and much easier on the eye, is the pathway made by sinking large pieces of broken paving into the lawn so that they lie flush with the grass surface. That is how I make my paths, and they have the virtue of being work-free when established, besides being easy on the eye. There is no tricky job of trimming path edges: the

(left to right) Chamaecyparis Boulevard; Chamaecyparis Ellwoodii; Corylopsis Pauciflora

Rose, Queen Elizabeth, makes a decorative hedge

mower glides smoothly over lawn and paving stones as if it were all lawn. An extra bonus in this style of path-making is that the path becomes part of the lawn instead of a separate feature. This is wonderful in a small garden, because it means that *no* space is taken away for paths.

Plan 1 on page 12 shows a simple outline of a back garden, fenced on three sides and laid out entirely as lawn, with site for garden shed and propagating-frame in one corner. (Plans 2, 3, and 4 show how this could be developed.) Paving stones have been let into the lawn to form a curving pathway finishing at the garden shed. From that point the path is a straight-sided concrete one. If you take that as a skeleton plan, with the proposed vegetable patch still part of the lawn, you have the beginnings of an easy-to-run garden, though it is not yet furnished. It is rather like a room with wall-to-wall carpeting, waiting for the furniture.

At this stage, you can see points that need watching. Where the lawn meets the concrete patch adjoining the house, and where the short run of concrete path divides the sites for shed and vegetable plot, there should be no step up or down. Lawn and concrete surfaces should be flush so that the mower can take the edges in its run. Watching such points helps to avoid making time-consuming jobs such as lawn edge-trimming. You still need to cope with the grass hard up against the fence. This you can do with the right mower, or a 3-inch (7 cm) strip along the fence can be treated with Weedol twice a year to defoliate the grass or with Superlec to retard growth. It is obvious that this skeleton could be improved by putting in some plants. We could do with something to hide or disguise the shed if one is put there – and one is almost certain to be needed.

If we have a vegetable plot we might like some form of screen to separate it from the area retained as lawn. A hedge would do, or a row of roses, shrubs, or some fruit bushes; or perhaps a trellis entwined with various plants. There are plenty of possibilities. That would still leave us with two stretches of bare fencing with grass growing right up to it. We might like to clothe the fencing (with rambler roses for instance) or to establish a hedge all the way along it. A good hedge could mean that if the fence began to crumble it need be replaced only by something small and inexpensive. The hedge would be the boundary screen.

The corners and edges of the lawn offer scope for cutting out segments and planting them with shrubs or flowering plants. We could cut a circle and plant a tree; either a spreading type to give shade or an upright grower to conserve space.

The skeleton plan gives a basis for a garden as simple and as easy-to-run as we care to make it, and yet completely adaptable. Above all, it gives us time. That simple skeleton provides a neat and habitable garden which can remain unchanged for as long as we take to make our decisions on furnishing it with plants.

By starting with the ground all lawn (or just call it grass) we can introduce any feature in easy stages. Instead of planting up an area of 100 square feet (9 sq. m) at once, we could first dig and plant just half that area and leave the remainder under grass for an extra year or more. This graduates the expense as well as the work, and the grass covering avoids any bareness while we wait for the completion of projected features.

There is probably no feature that demands less work than the garden pool, and yet it is a great attraction if well furnished with plants and fish. Water-garden firms will do your homework for you and supply the right balance of pond life to ensure that the plants and fish alike are happy, are keeping the water clean, and they need no attention. All you have to do is give the fish a little food at times. Nor is it difficult to install a pool, using modern methods and materials. This is not the place to go into details. The subject is fully covered in Chapter 10.

Perhaps we seem to be creating an instant garden with a simplicity of effort that takes your breath away. But when you recover your breath, you might well ask where that lawn came from if it needed so little effort. I said earlier that we should *think* of the area as all grass. You may remember also that I suggested playing for time, once the ground was cleared, by simply running a rotary mower over the surface regularly, say once a week.

Old grassland can soon be made into a play lawn (not a spectacular, ornamental one) by this treatment. But bare ground may be extremely slow to respond. In the wild, open country where I live a patch of ground laid bare would be smothered in weeds (including grass) within three weeks. And regular mowing would soon leave grass as the predominant weed. In other words, mowing would quickly create a grass patch, or a lawn of sorts. In the middle of a town the process would be extremely slow. Not many homes with gardens are being built these days in the middle of towns. Nevertheless, in an urban area we cannot expect nature to clothe bare ground as quickly as she would in open country. This leaves the risk that the area euphemistically described as 'lawn' in the plans discussed, may be a long time in growing a reasonable carpet, so that you must be practical. Either you put up with it patiently till nature has taken what time she needs to cover your patch or you need to do a bit of more orthodox lawn-making. Chapter 6 deals with the whole subject of lawns, so you can turn to that right away if you need to do so.

We have avoided complication by assuming that drainage and soil condition would not give us any problem. In the short term, we can continue to disregard these factors unless there are clear indications of drainage trouble, such as rain staying too long on the surface. In town and suburban gardens drainage is usually adequate because the local authority's drainage system carries away surface water. In country areas, where main drains are few and a long way apart, it can be a problem. Poor drainage in the garden is usually due to nothing more than compacted soil. Loosening subsoil with a garden fork will relieve such a situation. Lest your garden should need drainage, let me tell you how to deal with it simply, without elaborate and skilful pipe-laying. You need to dig a sump-hole 4 feet (1·25 m) deep on the edge of the damp area. Fill it with brickbats, bottles, and other firm, hard debris. Water draining into it will usually empty itself by seepage into the surrounding subsoil. Make a channel through the affected area to the sump-hole. The channel should slope gently, say from just over a foot deep at the start to 2½ feet at the sump-hole end (30–75 cm). It should be part-filled with the same sort of material as is put into the sump, and topped with about a foot of soil.

My garden had a patch where water used to stand on the surface in spring when the surrounding ground was dry. This, and the slimy surface, made it clear that drainage was needed. Crates of discarded wine-bottles were available from the off-licence shop to use as drainage material. I made a channel 20 yards (18 m) long and, since it was so long, I made it a foot (30 cm) deeper at the outgoing end than at the starting-point – starting at 18 inches and finishing at 2½ feet (45 to 75 cm). No sump was needed because the garden is on a high spot and at the outlet end of the drainage channel the water seeps out through a bankside on to the top of a slope which carries it away harmlessly. The trench was part-filled with the bottles, lying flat, and the aim was to top them with about a foot of soil so that light

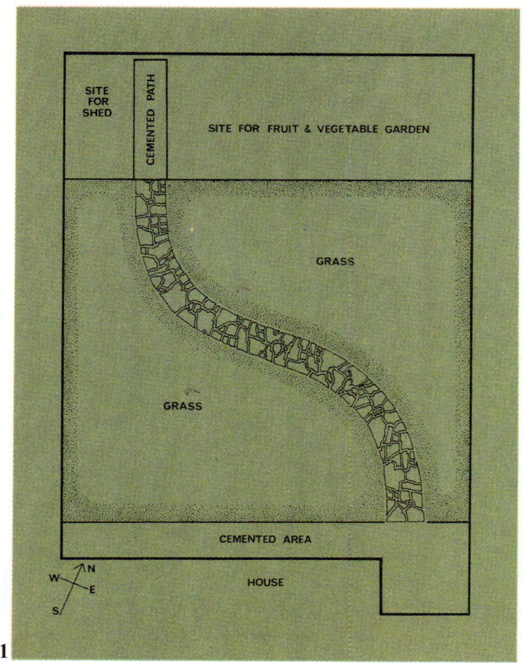

1

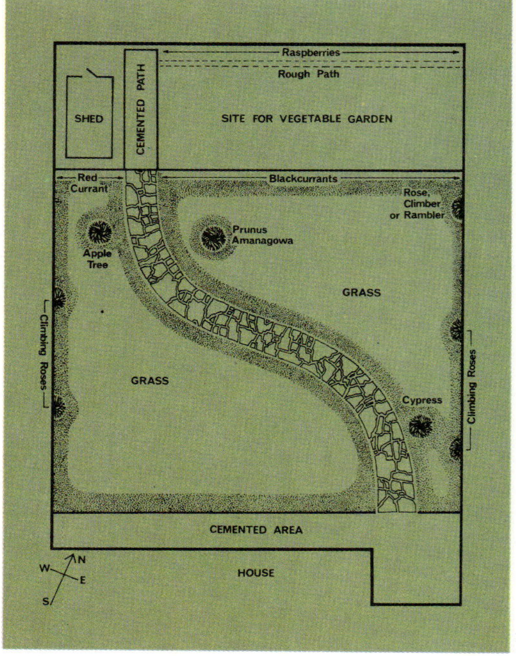

2

cultivation would not disturb the drainage material. Before the soil was put on, the bottles were covered with coarse material including thin branches and bits of folded wire-netting, and rubble, to help slow down settlement of the soil and thereby to keep enough space among the bottles for the water to flow.

With drainage worries sorted out, there is the general health of the soil to think of. A general fertilizer, applied at the rate prescribed on the bag, will be helpful. Fork it into the soil before planting is done. Clay soil will be improved by leaf-mould, peat, or sand; and sandy soil by leafmould or peat. Liming helps where vegetables are to grow. If it has too much clay or too much sand, the establishment of a fertile soil cannot be achieved by over-zealous digging, involving soil inversion. Inversion is the system of thrusting in the spade, lifting it out with a slice of soil on it, and turning the slice so that what was at the bottom of the spade is put on the surface while the former surface goes to the bottom. Fertile soil will die if buried under infertile soil. That is to say, lots of organisms will die in the lifeless surroundings. Soil depth can be increased only gradually, by working it just a little deeper each year – and not by ruthless inversion.

Everything considered up to this stage applies whether the site is flat or sloping. But the sloping site adds interesting possibilities. Take the garden pool, for instance. We could have two small pools with water flowing down the slope from one to the other. With a steep enough slope, we could have a waterfall. Such a feature would demand an electric pump which is neither difficult nor expensive and this could work a fountain.

But down to earth. The site on a slope may be changed into two flat areas on different levels with steps or a ramp connecting them. This is called ‘terracing’. The slope could be retained entirely or there could be a compromise, terracing the ground but allowing a degree of slope on one or both terraces. Whatever you do, don’t look on a sloping site as a handicap to your planning. I should not like a

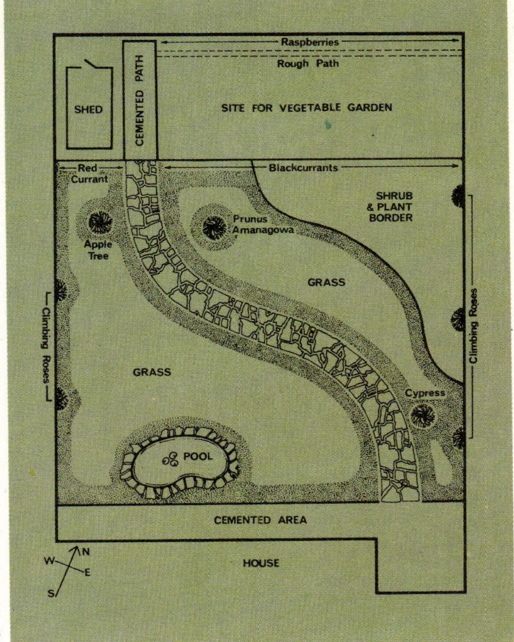

3

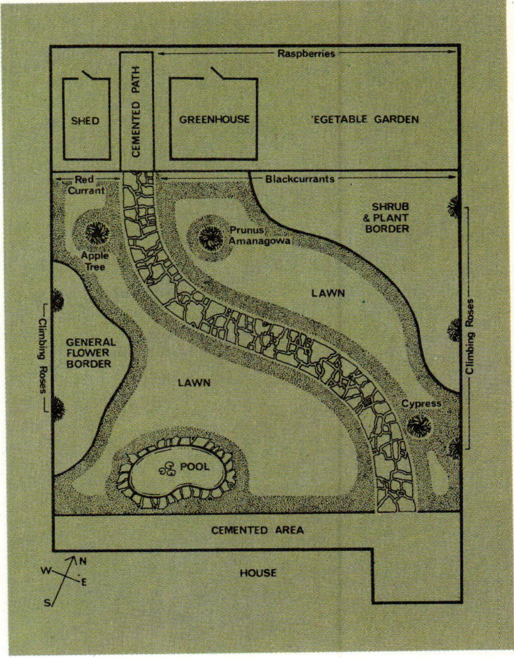

4

garden the size of mine to lie on one flat uninteresting level. Slopes, dips, and curves greatly improve garden outlines if there is room to exploit them.

Even in a small garden consider a tall hedge at the top of the slope, and a clear gap in the screen to create a vista. It is exciting and makes the garden seem much bigger. At the bottom of a slope imagine a screen of the right height, properly placed, revealing only the tops of shrubs and trees in gardens beyond. It creates the illusion of a long garden stretching into the distance. Terracing opens the way for breath-taking features. On the lower level we cannot see everything on the upper, so we can create surprises such as having an exotic feature which comes into view suddenly as we ascend.

In the front garden some planting should be done immediately. The tendency is for front gardens to be enclosed, by the house itself, and the front and side fencing or walling. The carpeting should be lawn where there is room to operate the mower comfortably and this calls for proper lawn-making. Usually a 2-foot-high (60 cm) wall, topped by 2 feet of wooden fencing separates the garden from the public footway. Stretching from this to the house one might find a fence 3 or 4 feet (90 cm or 1·25 m) tall. Along the house wall may run a 2-foot-wide strip of concrete linking up with the driveway, which may be of concrete, gravel, or tarmac.

In all, it is not an inspiring picture but it is neat and practical and can be dressed up to look attractive. Hedging is usually planted to disguise the fencing and for the busy man this could be of beech which will get by on an annual trim. The main feature may be a showy shrub such as a magnolia, or something neat, like a dwarf conifer. If the area is too small for easy mowing, the ground round the tree can be covered with gravel.

4 Taming the Wilderness

Normal delays over property transfer can cause a garden to be unattended for a few weeks before the newcomer moves in. During that time an attractive, established garden becomes a wilderness and looks a bit of a jungle through which the new owner is unable to find his way. Sometimes it may lie unattended for a longer period and the wilderness then becomes a major problem. If you are ever presented with that sort of overgrown garden, two things will strike you. First you will realize that planning a new garden from scratch is much easier than scratching a garden out of a mass of tangled growth. And soon afterwards you will realize that the chief natural obstacle to easy gardening is *weeds*.

This brings out a point I did not mention earlier, for good reason, when dealing with ideas for casual gardening. And the point is that there is really no such thing as a truly wild garden. The words contradict one another. A garden is a cultivated place, whether cultivated little or much, and so it cannot be wild. What is termed a wild garden is a place where wild plants are grown in conditions as near to their natural state as is acceptable to whoever is responsible for the garden. It is a place where the weed ceases to be a weed, but if cultivation is neglected it will again be a weed in the sense that it will be an undisciplined inhabitant of a wilderness. So what is a weed? It is often said to be any plant growing where it is not wanted. That oversimplifies the matter and is not the whole truth. Desirable plants sometimes become too big for the place where they were planted. Self-sown seedlings of cultivated plants may pop up where there is no room for them. To be a weed, a plant must have a nuisance value as well as being out of place. Its nuisance often enough is its power to survive under adverse conditions and its ability to scatter seed and reproduce itself all over the place.

When you have tidied up your wilderness, the task will be far from finished. There will be many more crops of weeds to contend with. There is a saying that one year's seeding means seven years' weeding. If you are pulling out weeds which are carrying seed-heads, don't wave them around. Carry them gently to avoid scattering

An overgrown lawn being cut with a Flymo rotary mower. This job must be taken slowly or the long grass will choke the machine and stall the engine.

Soil around newly-planted evergreen is made firm by treading.

the seed on the way to the compost-heap. Cut down and stack the weeds, keeping them clear of fences, and leave them to rot down. Where weeds are too tall to make this immediately practicable, just cut the weeds and let them rot where they fall. This will reduce their volume and make later stacking easier. Unfortunately, it will also deposit lots of seed, but the weed seedlings need not be allowed to grow to an unmanageable size before they are cleared. When the weeds and obvious rubbish have been cleared, you must resist the temptation to make immediate ruthless changes. Keep as much as possible intact until there is time to take stock and assess the whole garden. How long it takes depends on the season. It may even pay to see a year through and let every plant show what it is worth.

This need not stop the clearing out of eyesores and items clearly not to your taste. A misshapen tree or one that is far too big for its alloted space is a nuisance. Awkward steps can be replaced with a ramp where that is practical. Fussy brick surrounds or edgings are better cleared away because they harbour pests, besides impeding movement. You may well now be itching to get going with the secateurs, but again it is wise to go cautiously. Dead, damaged, and untidy growth should be removed from trees and shrubs and large cuts should be treated with a tree paint

Modern plastic ties make it easy to secure trunk of young tree to stout stake. Note that fastening shows no risk of strangling the tree.

to avoid their becoming infected. Complete removal of unwanted subsidiary branches should be the aim, rather than shortening any – unless you are certain what you are about. Cut so that no short snag is left; that is, remove neatly one arm of the 'Y' at the point where the unwanted branch begins. Bush roses are different. They can be cut back to about 1 foot (30 cm) tall if the time is anywhere between November and mid-April. Those who want to be more refined in their treatment of the roses should work to the general rule that the thicker and tougher wood needs fairly gentle pruning, while the weaker and thinner wood may be cut back more severely.

We have now reached the point where we have cleared up weeds and rubbish; removed any tree or shrub which had become a nuisance; removed also all fussy and ugly features; cut out dead wood generally and rough-pruned the rose bushes. If the lawn is cut, there is nothing more needing immediate attention unless the time is right for trimming any overgrown hedge. Light trimming of hedges is harmless at any time but severe pruning is not. Evergreen hedges which need to be cut back heavily should be done in May when the new sap is running. Severe cutting during winter can cause die-back and will make a gap in the hedge if the plant fails to recover. The best time to cut back overgrown deciduous hedges severely is in February.

When you survey the neat garden you have salvaged from the wilderness you inherited, you may not find it to your liking. It is not likely to fit into the skeleton layout described in the previous chapter. Do not worry; that layout was meant to illustrate certain principles, but those principles can be applied in varying settings. Aim at construction rather than destruction. Retain, adapt, and amend what you find rather than tear up and discard it.

In considering the new and empty site we dealt first with the back garden because that covered most of the points concerned in the layout of the small, orna-

Rose, Danse de Feu (climbing)

Chaenomeles, Crimson and Gold

mental, front garden. But in this matter of taming the wilderness, the front garden ought to have priority. After all, the passer-by cannot see into the back. Work so far suggested will have made the front garden look tidy, but not necessarily pretty. The way to raise your morale, as well as to create a good impression, is to bring in some sparkle and colour as quickly as possible. How quickly will be influenced by the time of year.

It is not a matter of major planning. As already suggested, that can wait. What is needed is a bit of instant gardening – introduction of a few colourful subjects. In summer this is easy because almost any garden shop will have what are termed 'summer bedding plants' in bloom or ready to bloom. They can be planted straight out without any worries about frost damage. Plants with distinctive colours set out in small groups at scattered points will make an astonishing difference. Take for instance three lobelias (blue), three alyssum (white), three geraniums (red), and three marigolds (orange). The first two subjects are cushion plants better used in positions near a path edge. Each group should keep to one subject and not be mixed. Three bright geraniums together will delight the eye, but a lone geranium in a mixed group would be lost.

In most months of the year your search for instant colour will probably take you to a garden centre where plants can be bought in root-containers so that they can be transplanted, container included, straight into your garden without fear of disturbance. At any season, these garden centres can supply plants which are in flower or ready to flower. If no outstanding flowering subject is available there are plenty of small shrubs with colourful foliage. There is a delightful little hybrid cypress which is a steel blue mixture. Its name is Boulevard, and more about it is given in the next chapter. At some seasons when instant colour is difficult, you can get subjects which come into bloom quickly. Bulbs of Colchicum autumnale planted in September will bloom in a couple of weeks. Their pale mauve flowers on

Rose, Golden Showers (climbing)

Rose, Message (climbing)

Hole being made with trowel to take plant raised in pot. Note how trowel is thrust into soil, then drawn towards the operator. This is easier than digging out a circular hole.

white stems stand up conspicuously in an autumn lawn. Bulbs of three tough dwarf irises planted in winter will quickly produce their brilliant miniature blooms – Iris histrioides (blue) in January, reticulata (purple) in February, and danfordiae (yellow) in March.

Where there are no wall-climbers, something should be planted as soon as possible, because these things take time to establish themselves. Even with container-grown plants from the garden centre, quick results are not easy against walls, and it might be preferable to have a plant dug up from the nursery in the normal way. A flowering climber is probably the best choice for the front of the house and most climbers need some support. I find that clematis will climb happily in a 2-inch (5 cm) mesh plastic netting called Netlon hung on cup-hooks on the wall. But a climbing rose is too strong for such a set-up and will lift the netting off the wall. Wall-ties, stout stakes, or trellis are needed for these roses. So we could hardly list them as ideal for easy gardening. There is one self-clinging flowering plant which is pretty enough for the front but it prefers a shady wall. It is Hydrangea petiolaris. Virginia Creeper and Ivy also are self-clinging subjects but I should prefer not to have them on the front wall.

Plant shown in picture above is firmed in after planting.

5 Clothing the Naked Earth

After all the dreaming and scheming, inevitably there comes a time when one must ask oneself the question: What shall I plant? And since we are aiming at casual gardening, the first essential in the decorative garden is a selection of shrubs, because they need little or no attention.

Shrubs, like wayward husbands claim to be, are often misunderstood. The suburban gardener and the professional have two totally different pictures in their minds when they speak of shrubs. The professional who is asked to design a shrubbery will probably require at least a quarter of an acre on which to lay out a good varied collection. He knows his shrubs, knows their sizes, and allots enough space for them to grow to maturity without overcrowding. The man with the average suburban garden may picture a shrub border about 4 feet wide and 10 feet long (1·25 × 3 m) holding a collection of about a score of shrubs. This book is not aimed at the professional, so the first picture is out. The second picture is out of focus and must be adjusted. The trouble is that most people think of a shrub as something about the size of a hybrid-tea rose bush, whereas many popular shrubs grow to man-height and more, with a proportionate spread. And while the professional thinks of shrubs as the backbone of a decorative garden, the home gardener finds it difficult to get a backbone of shrubs small enough to fit the body of his garden.

With these thoughts in mind I have selected shrubs small enough for the home garden but even if you have an extra large garden they will still suit you. In conventional gardening circles a small garden is one of half an acre or thereabouts. The term 'small garden' in this book may be taken to conform to modern ideas and to indicate something such as the garden of a semi-detached suburban house. In such a garden, sometimes referred to as the 'average garden', one can hardly talk of having a shrubbery any more than one would talk of having a separate rose garden or an orchard. Better just to think of a garden that makes good use of shrubs as a work-saving feature – planted singly, or in small groups, or in a mixed border with other subjects.

If we have that picture in mind it will help us to avoid making a bad choice, such as trying to plant over-large specimens or too many of them. Getting the right plant in the right place is perhaps more important with shrubs than with less permanent plants. Taking a rough definition of a shrub as a woody permanent plant with several stems coming from near the ground, we realize that it is bushy and if it grows tall it will cast a long shadow. So we have to consider where the shadow will fall, and choose the right aspect. 'Aspect' confuses some gardeners. What is called a south fence (or wall) is one having a southerly aspect, which means that it will be on the *north* side of your garden. In other words, when we define a garden border or fence in terms of compass points we refer to the aspect, the direction it faces, the direction in which you would be facing if you stood with your back to it. Other terms we use are 'warm' and 'cold'. A warm fence or border means one that gets plenty of sun (one looking south, probably) and a cold one

Azalea Amoena Coccinea

means one in the shade (probably facing north). In the small garden, aspect is not so critical as in the large one because small-garden fences are not usually too tall. However, it is a factor worth keeping in mind to help avoid such a mistake as training a rambler rose along the top of a north-facing fence. A rose so trained will turn its flowers towards the south, seeking the sun, and so will look at your neighbour instead of at you.

Spacing is perhaps more vital than aspect. It is essential to allot each subject the space it will ultimately need. This may look all wrong at first, with bare spaces, just as a cuddly little Old English Sheep Dog puppy looks lost in a kennel designed to house him all his life. But just as the puppy will grow and fill the kennel so will a shrub extend as it grows up. Shrubs grow more slowly than puppies but the bare spaces between can be filled temporarily without trouble or unnecessary expense.

There is an endless choice of seasonal subjects, besides longer-term plantings, that will fit in to give your garden a well-furnished look throughout the time that the shrubs are closing in towards each other. The distance apart to plant shrubs is at least half the sum of their diameters, so that a shrub with a spread of 4 feet in diameter and one with a 3-foot diameter need the centres of their planting holes to be at least $3\frac{1}{2}$ feet apart. And size here refers to their eventual spread, not to what they are at planting time.

Time for planting shrubs is generally from November to March because that is the period during which root disturbance causes least worry. But if you buy shrubs in pots, as offered

Chaenomeles Knaphill Scarlet
Deutzia Crenata
Deutzia Elegantissima
Pieris Taiwanensis

Spiraea Anthony Waterer

at garden centres, you can plant immediately whatever the month, because it can be done without disturbing the roots. In dealing with bare root plants, as distinct from container-grown ones, spread the roots fairly near the horizontal rather than pointing them downwards into the planting hole. The soil should have been improved by the addition of garden compost or peat. The hole should be deep enough to allow the shrub to sit at approximately the same level as it was in the nursery. Usually the old soil-mark on the stem is visible enough to guide you. Plant firmly by treading the soil, and stake temporarily if the specimen is tall or floppy. Tie by looping the tying material gently in a figure-eight shape round the plant and stake. Don't be afraid of strangling the stake: a tight tie there is needed.

In deciding where to plant, try to blend the subjects according to their seasons of beauty, so that at every season you will have a glimpse of something attractive. A winter-flowering shrub against the back wall of the house will be unseen if you never go into the back garden in winter. The mixture is improved further if the permanent plantings include herbaceous plants – perennials which die down to ground-level each autumn. Some suggestions are given later in this chapter. It is wise also to allow spaces for a few seasonal plants such as bulbs and annuals (*see* Chapters 7 and 9). Shrubs and perennials create a picture which is much the same one year as another. By splashing in a different selection of seasonal plants one can vary the picture, with different patterns of colour each year.

Another subject which can be brought into the mixture is heather. Apart from its virtues as a feature on its own, heather is a useful ground-cover plant which helps smother weeds, if plants are put 18 inches (45 cm) apart. It is another subject to consider for closing the gaps between the shrubs. Some notes on heather, with name of species and varieties are given on page 31.

Think of walls as well as the ground when you are planting a garden. Wall surfaces should be relieved by the introduction of plants to break up the outline and soften the corners. Free-standing plants will improve the appearance of the lower parts of walls but climbers are needed to clothe the upper areas. Many climbers need support to help them twine or to give their tendrils a hold. But there are some useful self-clingers, and these are the types for easy gardening. Best known is the ivy (botanical name: Hedera), a greatly underrated subject. There are several excellent ivies with different leaf sizes, and some with variegated leaves. Plant one near a wall and it will soon spread perpendicularly and horizontally without any support. The ivies are evergreen, and when they get a hold the wall is never bare. Also well known are the Virginia Creepers, whose leaves are colourful in autumn and whose stems are bare in winter. Incidentally the pattern made by the stems as they fan out on the wall, clinging securely, are quite attractive. A thicker-stemmed clinger, excellent for a sunless wall, is Hydrangea petiolaris, which produces corymbs of white flowers.

Climbers should not be planted right up against a wall, or the roots will dry out. Walls act like blotting-paper, drawing up the soil moisture. I plant about 2 feet (60 cm) away and lead the stem along the soil surface to the wall, putting in canes to protect the base of the stem from accidental damage.

In picking subjects to plant as eye-catching features, do not overlook Pampas Grass (Cortaderia argentea). This takes no maintenance and looks both stately and sub-tropical. The variety Sunningdale Silver is my favourite with long silvery plumes reaching up to 7 feet (210 cm) tall. Plant it where you will not brush against it, because its leaves can slash you severely.

TREES

It may not be easy to fit trees into the small garden, but I feel that every garden should have at least one tree, fruit-bearing or ornamental, to emphasize that length and breadth are not the only garden dimensions. Even in the tiniest of front gardens there is room for Prunus Amanogawa, the upright, flowering cherry which is slimmer than a poplar and has almond-scented soft-pink blossom. Trees of orthodox shape, which we call 'standard' or 'half-standard', are rarely under 12 feet (4 m) tall at maturity and often much taller. Their spread may equal their ultimate height. Find out before you buy, and allow room for the tree to grow up without becoming a nuisance. I suggest that the busy man's easy garden always has a little room for trees. I am also asking you (*see* Chapter 12) to make room for one or two fruit trees. For those reasons I am not going into details concerning trees, not even the so-called 'flowering trees' (species of fruits, such as cherries and plums, grown as decorative subjects rather than for fruit). I must not totally ignore subjects which are popular in many gardens, but please note the heights which I am giving and also to take note of trees you see in other people's gardens. You will soon see that space precludes their use in large numbers – except in really large gardens.

I mentioned earlier the upright Prunus Amanogawa, as my first choice in decorative cherries for small gardens. In the almonds, the favourite is still Prunus dulcis (also known as Prunus amygdalus) with its lovely pink blossom in March (20 ft: 6 m). Among decorative plums, I like Prunus cerasifera Nigra. Its pink flowers adorn leafless branches in March, and the leaves which follow are dark purplish (20 ft: 6 m). Since an upright habit of growth is a virtue where space is restricted, I think the popularity of the evergreen Cypress and its hybrids is well justified. Lawson's Cypress, otherwise Chamaecyparis lawsoniana, is available in many varieties. (It is easy to raise an interesting selection from seed.) You can get golden shades of this conifer as well as various greens. My choice is the variety Fletcheri, up to 15 feet (5 m) tall with a base spread of 6 feet (2 m). Its feathery, cypress leaves are a silver-grey-green.

While we are considering Cypress, I must mention two of my favourite dwarf varieties. Chamaecyparis lawsoniana Ellwoodii is said to grow up to near 10 feet (3 m). But I have some which have not reached 4 feet (1·25 m) after seven years (planted in grass). Ellwoodii has lovely grey-green foliage, and a multiple columnar shape. Chamaecyparis pisifera Boulevard is a beautiful thing. I was told it was slower than Ellwoodii but it is not so with me. Conical in shape, it has a broad base and bluish-green foliage which is really bi-coloured. Leaves are soft to the touch. This conifer grows in the shape of a pyramid 4 feet tall with a base 4 feet in diameter.

SHRUBS

In the shrub lists that follow, the plants have been classified into four seasons, but remember that seasons overlap; that they vary from year to year; and that they are influenced by local conditions of soil and weather. The flowering month is given where it is known to be fairly regular. Some items listed for autumn or winter are attractive at other times too, but that does not disqualify them for the places given them. A shrub's winter berries can be a bigger attraction than its summer flowers.

Potentilla Elizabeth

Viburnum Opulus Compactum

When using your catalogue look for 'A.G.M.' after the name of any plant and you will know that it is a winner. The initials indicate that the plant has won the Royal Horticultural Society's Award of Garden Merit, which indicates that a long trial at the R.H.S. Wisley Gardens has proved it a good performer under ordinary garden conditions. 'E' at the end of the description of a shrub signifies an evergreen.

Spring

Azalea. Large-flowered Japanese hybrids. These are of mixed breeding (mainly Kaempferi × Malvatica and Vuykiana). Their chief virtue is their mass of large blooms in May and June in a colour range embracing pink, orange, and red shades as well as white. They dislike lime. 4 ft × 4 ft (1·25 m × 1·25 m). Semi-E.

Chaenomeles japonica, the well-known 'Japonica' of cottage gardens. Can be trained as a wall shrub or grown as a bush. Its lovely scarlet blooms in spring are followed by quince-like fruits the size of golf balls. 4 ft × 4 ft (1·25 m × 1·25 m).

Cistus × corbariensis. A pure white Rock Rose flowering in May. There is also Cistus × purpureus which is rosy crimson. 3 ft × 3 ft (1 m × 1 m). E.

Corylopsis pauciflora. Opens its pendant racemes of scented primrose-yellow flowers in March before the leaves. Dislikes lime. 4 ft × 4 ft (1·25 m × 1·25 m).

Cytisus × kewensis. This hybrid broom is of prostrate habit and carries cream flowers in May. 1½ ft × 4 ft (45 cm × 1·25 m).

Hebe Autumn Glory

Pernettya

Juniperus Sabina

Deutzia × elegantissima. Fragrant flowers tinted rose-pink in May. Will thrive and flower freely in dry soil. 4 ft × 4 ft (1·25 m × 1·25 m).

Forsythia intermedia Lynwood. The brightest of the forsythias, with large, broad-petalled, rich yellow flowers which smother the branches in early spring. 6 ft × 5 ft (2 m × 1·5 m).

Mahonia aquifolium. Sometimes called the Oregon Grape. Formerly misnamed the 'holly-leaved barberry', which gives a clue to its character. Yellow flowers in February, followed by bunches of blue-black berries. 4 ft × 4 ft (1·25 m × 1·25 m). E.

Pieris taiwanensis. Young growths bronze. Lily-of-the-valley-like white flowers in March and April in fairly erect panicles. Dislikes lime. 4 ft × 4 ft (1·25 m × 1·25 m). E.

Prunus Cisterna. The purple-leaf sand cherry. Rich red leaves and white blossom in April. Can be kept fairly compact by light pruning. 5 ft × 4 ft (1·5 m × 1·25 m).

Rosmarinus officinalis. The common Rosemary, with grey aromatic foliage. Used as a herb. Grows up to 6 ft × 6 ft (2 m × 2 m) but is better kept cut back to half that size. E.

Salix repens argentea. A pretty willow with silvery-grey foliage. Yellow catkins crowd the leafless stems in early spring. Known as the Creeping Willow. 3 ft × 3 ft (1 m × 1 m).

Cotoneaster Conspicua Decora

Summer

Buddleia davidii nanhoensis. This is a dwarf buddleia by comparison, and has small leaves but carries the normal-sized spikes of mauve flowers in July. Attracts the butterflies. 5 ft × 5 ft (1·5 m × 1·5 m).

Caryopteris × clandonensis. Does not like a spot that lies wet in winter. Grey-green foliage, lavender-blue flowers in August/September. 3 ft × 3 ft (1m × 1 m).

Ceratostigma willmottianum. Blooms from July to October. Bright blue flowers. Light green foliage shows red tints in autumn. 3 ft × 3 ft (1 m × 1 m).

Hydrangea, Blue Prince. This variety of hortensis has blue flowers when grown on an acid soil or when treated with blue-ing agent. But is still pretty as a rose-pink bloom on non-acid soils. 4 ft × 6 ft (1·25 m × 2 m).

Hypericum calycinum. The Rose of Sharon. Some say it can become a weed. It certainly spreads well, and indeed smothers weeds, but is easy to control. About 1 ft (30 cm) tall, with large yellow blooms in July. E.

Philadelphus, Silver Showers. A compact form of Mock Orange. Has the usual strongly scented, orange-blossom type of white flowers in profusion in June. 5 ft × 3 ft (1·5 m × 1 m).

Phlomis fruticosa. The Jerusalem Sage. Silvery, sage-like leaves. Clusters of yellow blooms in August. 2 ft × 2 ft (60 cm × 60 cm). E.

Potentilla Elizabeth. Neat, spreading habit. Large canary-yellow flowers in June. 1½ ft × 3 ft (45 cm × 1 m).

Senecio laxifolius. Grey-leaved, dwarf. Likes to be cut back hard in March. Single, yellow flowers in June and July. 3 ft × 3 ft (1 m × 1 m). E.

Spiraea × bumalda Anthony Waterer. Easy grower of compact habit. Bright crimson blooms from June to October. 4 ft × 3 ft (1·25 m × 1 m).

Viburnum opulus Compactum. Makes dense bush with white flowers in early summer followed by shiny red berries which stay till autumn. 4 ft × 4 ft (1·25 m × 1·25 m).

Yucca filamentosa. Grey, sword-like stemless foliage. Tall spikes of scented creamy white flowers in August. 3 ft × 3 ft (1 m × 1 m). E.

Autumn

Cotoneaster. Several are suitable for the small garden and all are noted for their autumn berries. They include Cotoneaster conspicuus, 3 ft × 4 ft (1 m × 1·25 m); microphyllus, 2 ft × 3 ft (60 cm × 1 m); and salicifolius Autumn Fire, 15 ft × 5 ft (5 m × 1·5 m). All E.

Viburnum davidii. Good spreader. It is wise to plant a mating pair (male and female) to be sure of the lovely, egg-shaped blue berries in autumn and winter. 2 ft × 3 ft (60 cm × 1 m). E.

Hebe Autumn Glory. The hebes were formerly known as shrubby veronicas and may be listed under Veronica in some catalogues. This one starts showing its violet-blue flowers in summer, but they continue through October. 1½ ft × 1½ ft (45 cm × 45 cm). E.

Winter

Hamamelis mollis Pallida. This witch hazel is more dwarf and compact than others. The thin sulphur-yellow petals twist and form themselves into a ball which is unharmed by frost. 6 ft × 5 ft (2 m × 1·5 m).

Jasminum nudiflorum. The winter jasmine, with plenty of yellow flowers on its leafless, green branches. Best grown as a climber against a wall, where it is easy to train. But can be allowed to ramble over the ground.

Juniperus sabina tamariscifolia. Bright green foliage on branches which really hug the ground. Useful for the front of the border or alongside a path. 1 ft × 3 ft (30 cm × 1 m). E.

Pernettya mucronata. Another ground-cover. Has flowers like white heather in May/June followed later by clusters of marble-like berries. Needs lime-free soil and for good berries several to be planted. The berries on the variety Alba are pure white, while those on the Bell's Hybrids are pink and purple-red. 3 ft × 3 ft (1 m × 1 m). E.

Skimmia japonica Foremanii. A self-fertile form with bright red berries and handsome, leathery foliage. 3 ft × 3 ft (1 m × 1 m). E.

Thuja occidentalis Ellwangeriana Aurea. Golden foliaged, broad pyramid, looking handsome in winter. 3 ft × 3 ft (1 m × 1 m). E.

Viburnum × bodnantense Dawn. A hybrid. Winter-flowering. Clusters of deep-pink buds opening to soft-pink blooms, beautifully scented. 6 ft × 4 ft (2 m × 1·25 m).

HARDY PERENNIALS TO MIX WITH SHRUBS

There are two ways of using hardy perennials with shrubs and it is important not to confuse the two. One, which has already been mentioned, is simply a matter of filling gaps temporarily. The other is giving groups of perennials a permanent share of the border. In the first, the shrubs are spaced so that when they reach mature size they will be standing shoulder to shoulder and filling all the border. Whatever is put between the shrubs in their early years is only temporary as the shrubs ultimately crowd them out. There would always be room for other plants that would grow on as ground-cover and for small subjects which would be happy near the front of a packed border. The second method is more interesting and has become popular is some quarters. It involves giving shrubs and perennials fairly equal weight in the permanent scheme. Here, the perennials must be used in bold groupings, with a minimum of three in a group if they are big and far more in a group if the subjects are small.

The hardy perennials referred to here are hardy herbaceous plants sometimes called 'herbaceous perennials' and sometimes 'hardy border plants'. Their hardiness lies in the fact that their root system survives the winter though their leaves and stems die. Each spring fresh stem and leaf growth springs from the roots. Their life span varies, and in any event most of them need lifting and dividing every three or four years because they tend to get larger each year. They can be planted in autumn or spring. Before you enthuse too much over them, you should heed one warning, namely that they are difficult to weed by modern chemical methods, that is by the use of herbicides, which are great labour-savers in controlling weed growth among woody subjects such as trees, shrubs, and many sub-shrubby subjects like roses. It is not suggested that keeping the plants free from weed competition need be a major problem, but some weeding must be done by hand or with the help of a hoe. Nor is it wise just to choose casually from a list of your favourite perennials. The number that will thrive happily among shrubs is limited. Don't let me put you off planting a few of your favourites such as lupins and delphiniums if you feel keen enough about them. But they are not classed as mixing well with shrubs, and delphiniums do need staking, which is an extra chore.

Thuja Lobbii

Achillea, Golden Cloth

Although perennials are often bought as young plants from a nursery, many can be raised easily from seed sown outdoors in late spring or summer. Some subjects are slow to germinate and perhaps ought to be avoided by the gardener in a hurry. By 'slow' I mean that they may take six months. This does not worry me, as I often have shrub seeds which do not germinate till the year after sowing. My way with slow seeds is to sow in 3-inch (7·5 cm) pots and plunge the pots to the brim in a corner of the greenhouse border where they can be almost forgotten. Slow-movers to note include such popular items as aquilegia, helleborus, polyanthus, and primula. The list which follows is a selection I have made of hardy herbaceous perennials which are suitable for growing among shrubs.

Acanthus mollis, known as Bear's Breeches. The glossy, mid-green leaves are ovate with a heart-shaped base. Flowers are borne on 18-inch (45 cm) spikes. White and purple, July. 3–4 ft (1–1·25 m).

Achillea. The blooms, from June to Autumn, have flat heads. Try planting two or three species together. Example: millefolium roseum, pink and cerise, 2½–3 ft

Thuja Little Gem

Viburnum Tinus

Pyrethrum, Single Hybrids

(75–90 cms); filipendulina, var. Golden Cloth, yellow, 3 ft (90 cm); and ptarmica, var. The Pearl, white, 2 ft (60 cm).

Aconitum Bressingham Spire. A charming plant but note that all parts of it are poisonous. Flowers carried on tapering spikes. Violet-blue. July–August. 3 ft (1 m).

Agapanthus campanulatus. The African Lily, sometimes called Giant Bluebell. Hardier than many people think. Useful for planting in tubs. Blue. August–September. 2–2½ ft (60–75 cm).

Alchemilla mollis. Sometimes called Lady's Mantle. Has attractive leaves, hairy, palmate, and the star-shaped flowers have yellow-green calyces. Yellow. June–August. 1–1½ ft (30–45 cm).

Anaphalis triplinervis. Its grey-green leaves are covered on the undersides with woolly white hairs. Flowers, which have flat heads, are useful both fresh and dried, in flower arrangements. White. August–September. 1 ft. (30 cm).

Aquilegia (Columbine), Long-spurred mixed. Easily raised from seed. Flowers in

Scabiousa Caucasica

Helleborus Niger

a wide range of colours, May–July. 2–2½ ft (60–75 cm).

Astilbe × arendsii White Gloria (False Goatsbeard). Foliage is deep green and fern-like while the flowers are minute and are displayed in loose panicles. Does not mind moist or shady places. White. June–August. 2 ft (60 cm).

Bergenia cordifolia. Leaves are large, glossy, and leathery. Flowers are bell-shaped and form drooping heads. Although their time is spring, they flower beside a north wall in my garden in January. Lilac-pink. March–April. 1 ft (30 cm).

Chrysanthemum maximum (Shasta Daisy). The variety Little Silver Princess makes compact plants carrying large white daisies in July–August. 1½–2 ft (45–60 cm).

Helianthemum. Known as Sun Rose or Rock Rose, this is a sun-lover which should be cut back after flowering to keep it neat and encourage a second flowering in autumn. Various colours. June. 1 ft (30 cm).

Helleborus niger (Christmas Rose). Not well named. With care and protection it can flower for Christmas but is more likely to flower some time in the New Year. White. December–March. 1–1½ ft (30–45 cm).

Hemerocallis (Day Lily). The trumpet-shaped, lily-like blooms individually do not last long but the succession is so profuse that one does not notice. Many shades, chiefly yellows, oranges and bronze. June–August. 2–3 ft (60–100 cm).

Heuchera. Compact plants whose slender stems carry panicles of tiny flowers. Happy in any soil in sun or shade. Good for the front of the border and for cutting. Pinks and reds. July–August. 2 ft (60 cm).

Hosta fortunei albo-picta (Funkia, or Plantain Lily). Noted for its spring foliage. Young leaves, broadly variegated in yellow and green, go green by flowering time. Long somewhat tubular flowers on loose stems. Pale lavender. July–August. 1½ ft (45 cm).

Iris germanica. Of the wide range of irises, too great to cover here, this is perhaps the best known and easiest bearded iris. Its root is a corky rhizome which sits on the surface. There are many germanica hybrids in various bright colourings. Purple. May–June. 2–2½ ft (60–75 cm).

Kniphofia uvaria (sometimes listed as Tritoma) is the Red-hot Poker. Some kniphofias are known as Torch Lilies. Long, narrow arching leaves from the midst of which rise stiff stems topped by flower spikes which look like hot pokers. Various colours. July–September. 4 ft (1·25 m).

Lamium orvala (Giant dead-nettle). This plant thrives in any soil, in sun or shade, and does not spread. Leaves are mid to deep green. They and the flowers are rather nettle-like (without sting). Purplish pink. May–June. 2 ft (60 cm).

Meconopsis betonicifolia (formerly known as baileyi). The Himalayan Poppy. Flower stems should be removed in the first year, to prevent flowering; otherwise the plant might exhaust itself and die. It is an attractive upright grower. Sky-blue to lavender. June–July. 3 ft (1 m).

Monarda didyma. Known by several popular names including Sweet Bergamot. An easily grown bushy plant which flowers all summer and thrives in any soil, but prefers a fairly open position. Scarlet and other colours. June–September. 3 ft (1 m).

Nepeta × faassenii (often listed as Nepeta mussinii). Catmint. Planted at the front of the border it softens the outline of the border-edge. Small grey-green leaves. Tiny flowers on 6-inch (15 cm) spikes. Lavender. June–September. 1 ft (30 cm).

Paeony. Although this is not an easy subject, it is a beautiful plant with blooms which one might almost call exotic and is worth considering if you can spare a little patience for it. Plants of the herbaceous paeonies resent disturbance and are liable to sulk and refuse to bloom for a season or two after moving, which should be done in early autumn. However, even the leaves are attractive and they take on some lovely autumn tints. Flowers come in a range of delightful colours as well as white. The shrubby or sub-shrubby species are more difficult than the herbaceous paeonies.

Polygonum affine Darjeeling Red. Quickly forms a dense mat of dark green lanceolate leaves. Tiny bell-shaped flowers appear in close-packed clusters on 6-inch (15 cm) spikes. Deep pink. July–September. 9 inches (22 cm).

Pyrethrum. Good for cutting. Single mixed produce daisy-like flowers from June to Oct. in pink, rose, scarlet, crimson and white. 2 ft (60 cm).

Saxifraga × urbicum (London Pride). May be labelled Saxifraga umbrosa which was the original, but the hybrid is more vigorous so let us not complain. A cushion-like plant of fleshy rosettes with sprays of tiny flowers on upright stems. Pink. May. 1½ ft (45 cm).

Scabiosa Caucasica (Scabious). A good border plant, with flowers from June to October in shades of lavender blue and mauve. 3 ft (90 cm).

Sedum spectabile. Has flattish flower-heads which are 3–5 inches (7–12 cm) across and very big in proportion to the plants. Leaves are obovate, thick, fleshy, and pale green. Loves sun. Pink to crimson. September–October. 1½ ft (45 cm).

Stachys lanata (Lamb's Tongue). Perhaps of doubtful hardiness, but worth a try for its attractive pale green leaves with silvery downy hairs. Pink. June. 1 ft (30 cm).

HEATHER

Heather is easy to grow, spreads well to give good ground-cover, and is dense enough to smother weeds effectively. But many gardeners appreciate the extra virtue of its ease of propagation, that is to say, the ease with which stocks of plants can be increased. Apart from striking cuttings, propagation can be done easily by partly covering a clump with a peat-sand mixture in spring. New shoots will grow through the cover and root into it so that in October the clump can be lifted and the young plants pulled off for replanting. Heather is reputed to need a lime-free soil, but carnea, mediterranea, and × darleyensis are fairly lime-tolerant.

Species for summer and autumn flowering include the Grey Heather, Cornish Heath, and Scottish Heather or English Ling. In Bell Heather (Erica cinerea), popular varieties which flower from June to August are Apple Blossom with shell-pink flowers, and Golden Drop with pinkish-purple flowers and golden foliage. Of the Cornish Heaths (Erica vagans) the variety Lyonesse has white flowers from August to October.

Four varieties of the Scottish Heather or English Ling (Calluna vulgaris) which together will give colour from July to November are J. H. Hamilton, bright pink, July–August; Alba Plena, white, August–October; Mair's Variety, white, August–September; and H. E. Beale, pink, September–November.

The so-called 'winter-flowering' heathers all begin flowering in the winter months and carry on into spring. Outstanding among these are three varieties of Erica carnea – Winter Beauty, carmine, November–February; Springwood Pink, bright pink, January–March; and Springwood White, white with bright green foliage, January–March. Next come Erica darleyensis, variety Arthur Johnson, magenta, December–April; Erica carnea Vivelli, deep red with dark bronze foliage turning bright green in summer, February–March.

Meconopsis Baileyi

Aquilegia, Long Spurred Hybrids

Tritoma, Dobies' Hybrids

Heuchera Sanguinea

Stachys Lanata

6 Work and Play Areas: Lawns and Hedges

LAWNS

Generally speaking, a lawn is an area of grass kept neatly trimmed. Grass can stand frequent trimming, and since it is such a prevalent weed in these islands, any area of ground can be turned more readily into lawn than into anything else without sowing or planting. All plants can stand a degree of trimming during their season of active growth, providing there is always enough leaf area left on them. Without leaves, except during the rest period, the plant cannot live. If it loses leaves during the growing season it will try to replace them, but if it is repeatedly defoliated it will become exhausted. Grass does not mind having its leaves shortened, so it can be cut down low. Thus, by repeated mowing we can eliminate competing plants (weeds) and leave the grass. Coarse grass cannot stand being cut as short as a fine lawn, so short mowing will encourage the finer grasses. What we are left with after that is a mixture of grasses and a few weeds, such as daisy, dandelion, and clover, which survive the mowing. Passable, though not a quality lawn.

This, I hope, explains why ground which is regularly mown becomes a lawn of a sort. What sort of lawn depends partly on the nature of the ground (type of soil, quality of drainage, and so on), partly on how much weed is allowed to remain, and partly on how short it is mown. But it is unlikely that old pasture, or any self-sown grass patch will produce a lawn fine enough for a bowling-green. Therefore any attempt to produce a lawn without seeding or turfing should avoid being over-ambitious. A $\frac{1}{2}$-inch (13 mm) cutting height is short enough for the first season and perhaps even for always. No one species of grass can make a good lawn. Any mixture of lawn seed is a careful blending of grasses, and will vary first according to soil and situation for which it is intended, and next according to the purpose for which the grassed area is to be used. A purely decorative lawn can be softer than one which is to be walked on. A lawn for children to play on will have to be fairly tough. When you buy lawn seed you must choose the mixture to suit your needs and for a hard-wearing play-lawn the mixture must contain some perennial rye grass.

The site for a lawn needs to be free-draining, not to save roots from drowning but to save them from being suffocated. Wet ground quickly becomes compacted if frequently trodden. The result is to squeeze out the air. Nevertheless, for the busy person whose aim is easy gardening, I do not advocate the routine drill of thorough attention to drainage. Where there are no obvious signs of bad drainage – such as pools of water being too slow to go away after rain – I should take a chance and assume that drainage is satisfactory. If you make a wrong assumption you will know in due time, and you can leave the worrying till then. The essential preparation is reasonable digging, levelling, and raking. Although the object of this is to ensure that air gets to the roots, this does not mean pockets of air, such as are trapped among large lumps of soil. It means tiny air spaces between small crumbs of soil. So break it up into reasonably fine particles. Preparation for sowing involves treading to squeeze out air pockets and light raking to break up lumps which the treading may cause to form on the surface.

The easy way to sow is to scatter the seed on the surface and then rake very lightly in all directions until the seed is mixed into the top ½ inch (13 mm) of soil. You will never make it all disappear. However much you rake, some will be left on the surface. But do not worry. Between 1 and 1½ ounces to the square yard (40 and 50 g to the square metre) is the quantity of seed to use. Take half the total seed and scatter it so as to cover the whole area as well as possible.

With the remaining half of the seed, aim first at spots which seem to have been sown too thinly previously. Keep on sprinkling it wherever the covering looks too thin. When you have scattered all the seed this way, rake gently to mix the seed into the soil. This raking *must* be done in very short strokes back and forth, otherwise you could easily draw the seed into a heap instead of keeping it evenly distributed. Timing of sowing is important and early autumn is usually safest. Aim to avoid running into a spell of over-dry weather immediately after sowing. Showery weather is ideal. Don't choose the first dry day after a long showery spell, or the odds are that you will hit the beginning of a dry period.

After the gentle raking, the surface will be just a little too loose. Seed does better when it is hugged firmly by the soil. So the surface should be patted lightly with the back of the spade. Some people run a light roller over it, such as that on the mower, but this can be tricky, and patting is an easier drill for the inexperienced. When the grass is all through I *do* advise a light rolling with the mower roller before mowing. The emerging grass tends to lift the soil, and this needs firming again to hold the roots securely. The mower must be sharp for that first cut. A blunt mower tears the grass at any time, but where the grass is newly emerging a blunt mower tends to pull it out.

One thing which alarms many people when they sow a lawn is the number of weeds which emerge among the young grass seedlings. Most of these are annuals which die after the first mowing. After three or four weeks of normal mowing you will find that only a few stubborn weeds remain. These you can ignore till the grass is growing well – after three or four months. Even then, I do not advise treating the whole area with lawn weedkiller. Just apply the weedkiller to the weedy spots. Use only a lawn weedkiller. This sounds elementary, but I have known people use herbicides (which kill grass) when told simply to apply a weedkiller. Lawn weedkillers do not harm the grass (*see* Chapter 17).

When mixing a lawn weedkiller, never make it too strong. Use only the prescribed measure of concentrate in the proper volume of water. Overstrong mixtures scorch the leaves of the weeds, and the damaged leaves are unable to absorb an adequate amount of the hormone. The result is that although the leaves are damaged the roots do not get their full dose. The weeds survive and make new leaves. It is always safe to use a lawn weedkiller understrength, but folly to use it too strong.

Most gardeners like the new-mown lawn to show alternate light and dark stripes. These stripes are made by the roller, which is usually part of the mower. As the mower moves forward, its roller pushes the grass and bends it away. It stays bent rather than springing back to the upright position. As the roller goes away from you, the grass it is rolling looks paler because of the light it reflects. As the mower returns towards you it bends the tips of the grass blades in your direction so that the effect is less reflective, and darker. The stripe which looks light when seen from one end, will be dark when looked at from the opposite end. Are these stripes good or harmful? They do no good, but the rolling which creates them is helpful to the roots, providing the roller is not too heavy, and the rollers built into lawn-mowers are not. Since the bending does the grass no real good, it is wise to mow in different directions at different times.

But where does the busy gardener stand with all this? I think busy people today have no time for the meticulous work of giving the lawn its stripes. A rotary-type mower, with no roller, is easy and quick in action. That is why busy gardeners use rotaries. Mind you, a light rolling once or twice a year (beginning and end of season) helps to firm the grass roots and prevents development of bumps on the surface. Mowers are described in Chapter 18, but to help the beginner let me explain that a rotary mower is one whose cutters work with a propeller-blade action rather like an upside-down helicopter while the conventional mower (called a 'cylinder type') cuts by trapping the grass between a fixed bottom blade and a cylinder of spinning blades. This type of mower throws the grass forward and up into the air. The rotary sends the cut grass whizzing out along the ground, sideways or backwards according to the design of the deflector.

If you are in a hurry to make a lawn, you may be tempted to use turves. The idea that this is a speedy method is an illusion. You may have seen bits of decorative lawn made from turves at exhibitions, where obviously there would not be time to prepare them from seed, but such lawns are not intended to stay long or to take hard wear. Turfing for construction of a garden lawn is advised only where it is difficult to work the soil into a suitable condition for seeding. On clay soil, for instance, bedding down turf on a layer of sand will establish a lawn in reasonable time, whereas seed may not germinate well. Turves need time to get their roots into the ground under them and to bond themselves together. During that time they want careful rolling and watering, even if well laid. And good laying is not easy. So, I repeat, stick to seeding: it is the cheaper and easier way to make a lawn.

Lawn maintenance is not a big time consumer, but it is wrong to imagine that a lawn of rough grass needs less mowing than a fine lawn. Indeed the rough lawn made of coarse grasses produces heavier mowings than does the fine lawn. You make your own rules as to how often to mow. The extra-keen lawn man mows for effect. The busy man's aim is to make the job easy. The basic answer is the same in either case, namely that frequent mowing is your surest way to success. But the busy man must strike a balance between taking too much time by over-frequent mowing, and making the job hard through letting the grass grow too much between mows.

One of the Flymo range of wheel-less mowers which operates on a cushion of air and glides along as it mows

A reasonable frequency is once a week providing the mower is kept in good condition. But in warm, moist weather in midsummer it may want an extra cut.

Another tip is that if you mow at week-ends you should choose Saturday. If that day is too wet, there is a chance that you will get it done on Sunday. But if you make Sunday your regular day, a wet Sunday may set you back a whole week, and the job then will make you sweat.

For easy gardening there is no need to use a grass-box as a general rule. But where growth has got too long, the mowings can be a nuisance and can also encourage fungus troubles if left lying on the lawn in damp, cool weather. I have an area of what I call 'rough lawn', in which bulbs are naturalized. The grass is rather coarse and I cut it with a big rotary mower. Sometimes in warm, wet weather I have to rake off barrowloads of 'hay' after mowing, just through missing one cut. It certainly does not pay to miss a mow there, and I would not do so if weather did not defeat me. The purist will tell you to use the grass-box when there are weeds seeding in the lawn. This is to avoid spreading the weeds by scattering their seeds. But I think it is easier to ignore the weeds when mowing, and ultimately to clean them up in a routine lawn treatment. Your choice is either to risk a weedy lawn through taking it easy, or to use the grass-box to help control the weeds.

Apart from mowing and weeding, a lawn needs feeding, and treating for fungus diseases and attacks by worms and pests such as leatherjackets (grubs of Daddy Longlegs). This may sound a frightful load of chores but it is not. You can save time if you combine treatments so that they take perhaps half an hour two or three times a year. Try using a two-wheeled implement called a 'lawn spreader', the workings of which are described in Chapter 18. General lawn troubles are dealt with in Chapter 17 which covers pests, diseases, and chemical aids.

The shape of the lawn can cause difficulties. For instance, squared corners are awkward to mow. If you have such a hazard, the way to get rid of it is to round off the corner and plant some weed-smotherer in place of the grass you remove. Lawn edges which give on to bare soil look very untidy if not trimmed when the grass is cut. But lawn-edge trimmings can be hard work and should be avoided where possible unless you have a powered edge-trimmer. Wherever possible, I have hedges or plants growing where they hide the lawn edges. Edgings between lawn and path are avoided either by having a low hedge between lawn and pathway or by making the path of paving stones set into the grass. I avoid having a big drop from lawn to path or border, because thick edges tend to crumble. Any trimming of edges is done at an angle – never perpendicular, so that the edge will not readily crumble.

The Spintrim lawn edger; a powered, edging machine designed by Robert H. Andrews Ltd, of Sunningdale, Berks.

(left) The Qualcast Astronaut is a 14-inch (36-cm) conventional cylinder-type mower driven by mains electricity. (right) The Toro ride-on rotary mower.

HEDGES AND SCREENS

Lawn and path butting together make a junction line which can be a time-consuming feature. If you overcome this by putting a hedge along the dividing line, make the hedge a low and informal one that needs little or no maintenance.

In the decorative garden, lavender or hardy fuchsias make excellent subjects. True, a hardy fuchsia can grow into a large, tall plant but not if it is pruned fairly hard.

Let us consider hedging generally – boundary hedges, dividing screens, masking screens, and decorative reinforcements. I would normally say that the old favourite evergreen, privet, has no place in the busy man's garden because it needs regular trimming. But some people would disagree because they use electric hedge-trimmers. Hedges are shockingly neglected in gardens. They are planted in unprepared soil and left to fend for themselves except for trimming, which is usually done badly. Privet is a ravenous feeder, which is why it suffers more than most subjects from this neglect. Privet should not be grown along the back or edge of a plant border of any kind because it will forage and steal nourishment intended for the other plants. When newly planted it should be cut down to half its height to encourage bushy growth. It should be trimmed regularly throughout the season, should be shaped like a wedge, thin end at the top. The reason for keeping it slim and wedge-shaped is partly to let in light without which the twigs would be bare. The wedge-shape also reduces the risk of damage from the weight of heavy snow.

The ground for all hedges should be prepared as for other plantings, which means that the soil below root-level should not be impermeable and the soil

No garden is too big for this Australian ride-on mower with its 7 h.p. engine (8 h.p. optional). It is called the Deckson Ride-on Rotary.

above root-level should be crumbly and fibrous. (Adding peat or leafmould helps make it fibrous.) A dressing of general garden fertilizer should be worked in at the rate prescribed on the bag. In late winter or early spring each year, when the planted garden is being fed, include the hedges in this treatment.

If you want a barrier against strong winds, the best subjects for garden hedges are laurel or holly. Most people think these are slow but this is not strictly true. They are slow for the first couple of years but after that they grow rapidly – in both height and spread. They are tidy growers which do not go straggly and you can get away with trimming them only once a year, in August or early September. I have a hedge of holly and laurel planted alternately. It stands on the eastern edge of the

The Qualcast Jet-Stream is a 15-inch (38-cm) mains-electric rotary mower with rear-mounted grass-box.

(above) Wheeled spreader for applying fertilizer or combined fertilizer and weed- or mosskiller to lawns.

(below) Mains electric hedge-trimmer in use. Note that the flex is led safely over the shoulder of the operator, and cannot get in the way of the cutting blades.

plateau on which the house is built and it filters the cold east winds of winter and early spring when they come sweeping up from the long orchard.

Where taller screens are required the need is usually more obvious, whether it be a matter of blocking out an unsightly view or providing privacy. For this sort of job, the various cypresses are good. They are not too expensive if you buy hedging specimens and not those selected to stand as individual trees. Planted 4 or 5 feet (1·25 or 1·5 m) apart, they make a wonderfully dense screen which can be headed back to any reasonable height. They grow 2 or 3 feet (60 cm or 1 m) a year after the first year. And, incidentally, it pays to be patient and economical by buying small ones (about 2 feet high) because they settle better than bigger specimens. There is a big hybrid cypress called Cupresso-cyparis Leylandii (or Leyland's Cypress) which grows about twice as fast as the average, but I think it is too big for small gardens. I grow one as a specimen just to compare it with neighbouring trees of Lawson's Cypress and others I have raised from seed. Lawson's Cypress needs hardly any attention once planted.

TRAINING BEECHES

The top of a beech hedge should not be trimmed till the desired height is reached. Early trimming will slow it and will not make it bushy. A beech hedge is an exception to the normal pruning rules for deciduous hedges. Its main trim should be given in August, though light snipping to tidy up the side growths can be done at any time. August pruning gives the beech time to settle down and not feel shocked. That way, it retains its leaves all winter till the new spring growth pushes them off. They go brown and dry, of course, but they are attractive, and branches well clothed in dry leaves look much better than bare twigs.

Hedges have various uses in gardens. They can divide one section from another or give a snug backing at a spot where we hope to put the deck-chairs. These hedges do not have to be tall, unless we have reasons for growing something tall: for instance we may want runner beans and it may be convenient to grow them as a dividing hedge. Usually it is just a matter of providing something to break the view so that when we sit on the lawn we are not gazing at the brussels sprouts.

But whatever the need, it does not have to be purely ornamental. Various soft fruits are easy to grow and can serve the dual role of providing screening while having a cropping value in addition. Raspberries, gooseberries, red currants, and blackcurrants are subjects which I grow as hedges because they save space when grown that way. Apples or pears also can be trained as hedges but they are not so easy because training and pruning call for care and skill. They look smart when well grown as cordons or espaliers but I do not commend the idea to any but truly skilled gardeners. (*See* Chapter 12 on fruit.)

A line of shrub or floribunda roses makes a colourful divider and there are several flowering and berrying shrubs but they need more space than the other subjects I have mentioned, and they really belong to the bigger garden. Sometimes a hedge is wanted more for its decorative than its screening value. Something colourful along the edge of a path, whether it be tall shrub roses or low-growing lavender, can be a feature in its own right. If you use a row of annual flowering plants you have the advantage that you can change your mind each year. For this sort of hedge you have merely to look for annuals which grow the height you want and which need no staking. Lavatera (mallow) is perhaps the best example, especially for a sunny position. It grows between 3 and 4 feet (1–1·25 m) tall and the variety Tanagra carries lovely blooms in cerise-pink, 3–4 inches (7–10 cm) in diameter. The flowers are useful for cutting. Another annual which I like as an outline-breaker along a path edge is Cosmos. It is not so tall as lavatera – up to 3 feet – but it is delightfully informal with feathery foliage and blooms of mixed colourings.

USEFUL SCREEN

For the double purpose of hiding the compost-heap and providing something to eat, I like Jerusalem artichokes. The edible part is the root, which is nobbly and has a smokey flavour. The stems and blooms are like sunflowers. Tubers planted in February grow steadily to produce a 6-foot (2-m) screen which needs no staking. Eat what roots you need and save a few to plant the following year.

The hardy fuchsia has many uses, including that of flowering hedge. Nearly all hardy fuchsias can survive outdoors all winter except perhaps in very cold, wet areas, but the varieties classed officially as 'hardy' in fuchsia language are those which are earliest to come out of their winter rest and start to bloom. The fuchsia is a sub-shrub whose woody stems may die down in winter like those of herbaceous perennials. But they rarely behave that way once they are established. It is helpful to draw up soil to cover the bottom 4 to 6 inches (10–15 cm) of stem in winter. It is best to start a fuchsia hedge with young plants in June. Keep nipping out the tips of young shoots till the plants make a bushy shape.

Battery-operated hedge-trimmer by Black & Decker does all the work of a full-size mains-electric trimmer. Useful where a hedge is a long way from a power-point or for people who prefer not to have a trailing flex.

Choose your varieties from this list of hardies:

Army Nurse, red and blue
Brilliant, rose scarlet and rose purple
Chillerton Beauty, white edged pink/violet
Dorothy, crimson and violet
Eleanor Rawlins, two shades of red
Florence Turner, pink and purple
Howlett's Hardy, scarlet and purple
Joan Cooper, rose-opal and cherry-red
Lady Thumb, red and white
Mme Cornelissen, scarlet and white
Magellanica, red and purple
Mr A. Huggett, cerise and pink
Mrs W. P. Wood, pale pink and white
Mrs Popple, scarlet and violet
Nicola Jane, red and pink
Phyllis, two shades of pink
Peggy King, rose and purple
Riccartonii, scarlet and purple
Susan Travis, two shades of pink
Thompsonii, scarlet and purple

PLANTING PROBLEMS

Experienced gardeners do not always agree on the best time for planting trees and shrubs, whether for hedging or for general garden decoration. No strict rule applies. One has to consider type of ground, its temporary state (over-wet or over-dry), the weather, and the object of the planting. The general rule is that deciduous subjects are planted during the dormant season (November–March) and evergreens in early autumn or late spring. Conifers are generally treated the same way as deciduous subjects.

These rules are based on the need to reduce the transplanting shock. A deciduous tree does not feel much shock if planted during its resting season (November–March). An evergreen never rests completely but maintains a tiny flow of sap all winter to hold on to its leaves. The shock to an evergreen is least when transplanting is done as the sap flow is falling (September–October) or as it is rising (April–May). There are other factors which affect planting dates. If the soil is heavy, cold clay, late planting (March) is usually better because it spares the roots a winter of cold feet, and it offers them warmer, lengthening days during which to settle in. On light, sandy soil, this late planting can be a disadvantage because growth may go faster than re-rooting. So on such soil it may be better to plant in November. An obvious local factor is the degree of exposure to prevailing winds. More trees and shrubs fail through being dried out by cold winds than through winter frosts. The remedy is to put up some temporary screen, such as polythene sheeting, where needed, and to make sure that the soil at the roots does not dry out. Ground should never be planted when it is either completely dry or extremely wet.

My own opinion is that the best time to plant holly, laurel, or cypress is late March or April. Beech, I like to get in a little earlier if the ground permits (mid-February on). Once you *know* the rules, you can adapt them to suit yourself. After all, you want your plant to be happy. See that it does not suffer dehydration due to exposure to drying winds or hot sun. See that its roots are moist but not drowning.

One major simplification when you want a shrub or tree nowadays is that you can buy it from a garden centre. That is the part of a plant nursery where plants are offered for sale in pots or the equivalent. These are growing plants, not uprooted, sleeping specimens. Their root-containers can be ripped away and the plant can be placed neatly in the ground without any shock or root disturbance. This operation can be carried out at any time of the year, so there is no need to worry about planting seasons. But this would be expensive for a hedge of moderate length. Hence the drill for normal planting has been explained.

7 Outdoor Bulbs

For maximum effect from minimum effort, there is nothing to beat bulbs growing in lawn or rough grass. Once planted, the bulbs can be left entirely to their own devices – no feeding, weeding, watering, pruning, staking, spraying, or any of the operations required by some plants. And for their part, they will not only bloom well but will multiply in number. True, we are advised usually to snap off the seed-heads when the flowers fade. The object is to save the bulb's energy which would otherwise be consumed in producing seed. But I never bother, and the grassed-over bulbs seem to do better each year. On the lawn, I take the trouble in summer to chop down the dying leaves of the bulbs. But this is a simple job and doing it makes a great improvement in the look of the lawn.

Leaving bulbs to their own devices is termed 'naturalizing', because it means allowing them to grow the way they would do naturally. Some of mine do just that. One side of my drive is covered with bracken for most of the year. Every spring it is a mass of daffodils and narcissi which stand up on the carpet of dead brown bracken leaves. When the daffodils are finished and their leaves start going brown, up come the new green shoots of bracken, and the rest of the season is theirs. It is an excellent arrangement. The bracken smothers weeds which might attempt to invade, and its dead leaves keep the ground snug all winter, besides helping to nourish the soil so that it can keep my daffodils happy. My total annual labour there is precisely nil. No gardening could be easier than that. On the lawn, there is that little job of tidying away the dying leaves, but that is the only work the bulbs give me in the whole year, and even that could be left if I did not think it would look too untidy amid the mown grass.

Bulbs can be naturalized in open soil, among shrubs for instance, but they do not look good unless they are weeded occasionally. And this creates a problem because any garden tool used in the soil is liable to damage the bulbs, which in turn brings the risk that disease may attack the damaged tissues and spread to other bulbs. Herbicides can be used for weeding but one cannot help worrying, however wrongly, at the risk. The best way is under grass.

Like other work-saving features, the flowering lawn, created by growing bulbs in the grass, involves the initial planting, but this is not much if you time it well. The time I choose is November, despite the fact that daffodils prefer September or October planting so that they can do a bit of rooting in the warmish soil before their winter sleep. November is the best month for turf-laying and since turves have to be lifted for the bulbs to go under them they have to be relaid. Turves disturbed in September or October may run into trouble in a dry spell, whereas there is no such risk in November.

Bulb-planting in grass must be in informal groups or the effect is too stiff. The oldest known way of achieving this effect is to load a shovel with bulbs, sling them off with a swinging action, and plant them where they fall. But since the turf will have to be taken up, the job is not so easy that way because while the turves are

Chincherinchee

Muscari Blue Spike

being lifted the bulbs have to be moved from where they fall. One could plant them alongside where they fall and still retain the pattern, or one could simply turn up a large patch of turf and do the scattering on the bare soil. I suggest the latter method. The scattering, whose object is just to produce an informal grouping, can be done in double handfuls. Before planting, lift off or roll back a patch of turf then loosen the soil beneath and fork in a dusting of bonemeal. Put daffodil bulbs 3 inches (7 cm) below this soil surface and replace the turf. The same depth would do for colchicums, while crocus and snowdrops would need only light covering.

I have colchicums in the same lawn as the daffodils so that this lawn gives two flowering displays each year, in spring and autumn. It would be easy to add crocuses and snowdrops, but one must not overcrowd a lawn or mowing becomes difficult. As it is, there comes a spell in early summer when the mower has to dodge large, flowerless clumps of leafy growth of daffodils and colchicums. If you wonder why daffodils and colchicums are in full leaf at the same time despite the fact that one blooms in spring and the other in autumn, the answer is that their habits differ greatly. The colchicum produces leaves without bloom during the spring and early summer. These die and then the blooms appear, without a sign of leaf, in late summer/early autumn. The slender white stems and crocus-like flowers of Colchicum autumnale are known as Naked Ladies – simply because of the absence of leaf. The blooms fade and die in October but the bulbs should be left in the ground. Their leaf growth the following spring is essential to the recharging of the corm ready for its next flowering. (Daffodils produce their leaves at

Crocosmia masonorum

Crocus (Striped Beauty, Giant Purple, Golden Yellow, Snowstorm, Queen of the Blues)

Iris Mixed

Hyacinth Mixed (in window-box)

flowering time, in spring.) All this indicates that November is not the normal time for planting colchicums, although that is the time I have suggested for planting them in lawns. The drill is to plant the colchicums temporarily in spare ground when they reach you in July or August, marking the spot carefully with short canes. Let them flower. Dig them up in November and replant immediately in the lawn.

There are several classes of narcissi and many varieties of the large-trumpet type we call 'daffodils'. For the beginner I suggest buying what the catalogues call a 'collection'. This is a group of varieties selected by the grower. Collections suitable for naturalizing are usually a good buy.

So far in this chapter on outdoor bulbs I have concentrated on two items because I am hoping that the thought of a colourful lawn will arouse your enthusiasm, and

I wanted to show you first how easy it is. Before we move on, we ought to consider a few points about what we call 'bulbs'. For simplicity, we talk of garden 'bulbs' when we are concerned with more than strictly bulbs. Sometimes we spell them out as 'bulbs, corms, and tubers', but among the so-called 'tubers' we include some tuberous roots which are not true tubers. Generally, the differences need not concern us, but sometimes getting them into the right category can help us to understand their cultivation better, and do it more easily – which is part of the aim of this book. Let me give my own definitions, in terms as simple as I can.

Bulb. A bulb is a micro-plant packed in a natural food-store. You can see this if you slice a bulb in half from bottom to top. The shape of the flower-bud will be clearly visible in the centre.

Corm. A thickened portion of stem; another natural food-store, containing the wherewithal to make stems, leaves, and flowers (just as a seed does).

Tuber. A swollen root, usually having 'eyes' from which new shoots will spring to make a new plant.

I don't think the casual gardener need worry much about the differences between bulbs and corms. But there is a vital difference between a true tuber and a mere tuberous root. The tuber (potato for example) makes shoots, from its eyes, to produce new plants. But a tuberous root, such as that of a mature dahlia, cannot. Its growth comes from the base of the stem, so it is important not to treat the roots like potatoes and break pieces off in the vain hope that they will grow.

One thing bulbs, corms, tubers, and tuberous roots have in common is that they can be stored 'dry'. Since water is part of their make-up, they must not be allowed to dry out completely. They must be stored cool, since a warm atmosphere is usually a dry one. But in cool storage conditions we have to watch for dampness created by the condensation which comes when warm air creeps in and strikes the cold surfaces. All 'bulbs' in store should be checked regularly and dusted with sulphur or other mildew repellent if needed. All subjects we find in the bulb catalogues are light on time and labour, unless they are used for large-scale displays involving regular replanting. Tulips are often planted that way, but this mass planting is not essential. They can be dotted round in small groups among other things in a border, which is the way I advise for work-free gardening.

Crocuses and snowdrops can be naturalized in lawns, but if you take the advice given earlier in this chapter you will stick to daffodils and colchicums. Do not switch the left-over items to your back lawn, because only a decorative lawn, not a play lawn, is really suitable for bulb-planting. The blooms, and the leaf growth, are a nuisance on a lawn where you want to play or lounge. However, the fact that bulbs will grow well in grass makes no difference to their value for growing elsewhere. A few snowdrops and crocuses should be popped into the ground near the front door or window to give you cheer in the bleak, perhaps snowy days of late January and February.

Dahlias. It ought to be more widely known that apart from the named varieties in the several classes of dahlia there are attractive dahlias which one can raise from seed. One can buy seed to suit broadly one's choice – for example cactus-flowered, decorative, or pompon – but naturally the seedlings will vary in colour and will not have varietal names. Seed is not expensive and seedlings raised early by starting under glass in January, February, or March will flower in their first year. Those raised later without the help of a greenhouse will make tuberous roots which can be taken up and stored for planting the following year, when they will bloom. All who like raising plants from seed should try these, because besides the saving in money there is the fun of finding some quite exciting specimens in any batch of seedlings. (Seed sowing is dealt with in Chapter 16, on propagation.)

Dahlias can be bought as plants, or as roots called 'pot tubers'. To produce these tubers, the nurseryman has had to keep plants growing till they have formed the swollen storage root, so they cost a little more than the simple rooted cuttings or 'green plants' which one buys in June. The problem of choosing varieties is made difficult by the fact that there are ten broad types or classes of dahlia – single, anemone-flowered, collarette, paeony-flowered, decorative, ball, pompon, cactus, semi-cactus, and miscellaneous – and these classes are split up according to size: giant-flowered, large, medium, and so on. This classification can be deceiving. You might for instance want neither giants nor large blooms so you choose 'medium'. Then you discover that a medium-sized dahlia bloom may go 8 inches (20 cm) in diameter; and even a miniature may be up to 4 inches (10 cm) in diameter. Don't let me put you off the 'medium' sizes. There are too many good varieties in this range for you to ignore them. And the size of bloom does depend on a few tricks of feeding and disbudding, so that they do not reach top size in the average garden.

I plant out dahlia roots in late April in enriched soil in a sunny position. Enriching means working peat, leafmould, or garden compost into the soil, as well as feeding with a general fertilizer. If you are in a hurry you can neglect a bit of this generous treatment and still get passable blooms. They grow up to 4 feet (1·25 m) tall and staking is vital as the dahlia makes a big heavy plant which is vulnerable to wind damage. String or other tying material should be tied tightly to the stake but looped lightly, not tightly, round the plant. Frost blackens the plants in autumn, and after this blackening I allow a couple of weeks before digging up the roots and storing them in a dry, airy, frost-proof building.

In the first stage of storing I cut the stems down to 6 inches (15 cm) and stand the roots upside-down to avoid collection of moisture in the base of the hollow stems. When they are reasonably dry, the roots are stored away. They are checked occasionally for signs of mildew, which is treated with Dithane or other mildew control. The following April the tubers are planted out – big ones being divided – and the sequence begins again. Dahlias classed as 'decorative' are those with broad petals. 'Cactus' types have petals which roll lengthwise and look spiky.

Gladioli corms come normally in sizes from 10 centimetres to over 14 centimetres in circumference. Most popular is the 12–14 centimetre range. Catalogues offer much choice in what are classed as 'Large-flowered'. These may be marked 'E', 'M', or 'L' to indicate whether they are early, mid-season, or late. Earlies bloom about 90 days after planting; mid-season, 100 days; and lates, 120 days. Whatever their season, I plant in batches from late March to mid-May to spread the season of bloom. Besides the Large-flowered class, there are the Butterfly Gladioli and a new type called Coronado Gladioli. Butterfly grow as tall as the Large but their flower spikes are more dainty, their flowers smaller, and they are more suitable for use as cut flowers. Their corms are smaller and the 10–12 centimetre size is ideal. Coronado Gladioli are the result of crossing an early, small species with a Butterfly variety and earliness is one of their qualities. They grow about 3 feet (1 m) tall with elegant spikes of dainty flowers and, like the Butterfly varieties, they are excellent for cutting. Their corms are smaller and the 8 centimetre size will make strong plants. Coronado have the extra attraction of

Double Daffodils (Golden Ducat, Irene Copeland, Mary Copeland, Texas)

producing two or three stems to a corm. They stand without support except in exposed positions.

Both Butterfly and Coronado are bought usually as mixtures and in each case a good colour range is assured. Large-flowered are bought as named varieties, but collections are available and these are good. Mixtures too are often offered and these are a good investment for cutting. Start planting in the second half of March, or as soon afterwards as frost is out of the ground. Plant more at fortnightly intervals to prolong the display. When growing for cut flowers, plant 9 inches (22 cm) apart in rows and allow 3 feet (1 m) between rows. In the flower border, corms should be planted in groups, preferably of one variety, and corms should be 6 to 9 inches (15–22 cm) apart. When you dig up your gladioli corms in autumn to store them away, safe from winter frost, you might like to know that they are not the ones you planted. A new corm forms during the season just above the old, at the base of the stem, and the old corm dies. To allow room for this natural replacement process, corms must be planted 4 inches (10 cm) deep. At this depth, good drainage is essential because the dying corm could be prone to rot if it is lying in waterlogged soil.

Decorative and cactus dahlias are colourful border plants.

Lilies have one fault: they sometimes sulk. The bulbs do not like being disturbed and they are inclined to show resentment by taking a year to settle in. Planting time can be either November or March, but the spring date is safer on cold soils. Whatever the timing, you should not leave bulbs lying around. Plant them as soon as you receive them. A large number of lilies are what is termed 'stem-rooters'. These make normal roots at the base of the bulb, but as the stem grows they make a second root system above the bulb, at the base of the stem. It is vital that bulbs of stem-rooting lilies should have enough soil over them to accommodate the stem roots. The general rule is that the bulb should be planted two and a half times as deep as its diameter. And the rule for stem-rooters is to have 5 inches (12 cm) of soil on top of them after planting. This depth can take the bulb into a damp layer unless the ground drains reasonably. One way with stem-rooters is to put extra soil round the stem as the plant grows. This is a good method, but for the busy man I naturally advocate putting the bulb deep enough to avoid the need for extra soil. Although the flowers are happy in the sun, the roots like cool ground. A good compromise is to plant the bulbs among low-growing shrubs which will keep the ground shaded. Stem-rooters are indicated in the list given later in this chapter.

Tulips are classed in 'divisions' of which there are several, apart from the species. Of the species, all of which have hybrids, the three chief ones are the Kaufman-

(right to left) Dahlias: Hamari Girl, giant decorative, light rose-pink; Go American, giant decorative, bronze; Silver City, large decorative, white; Corton Trudy, giant decorative, clear yellow

niana, 4–9 in. (10–22 cm), which bloom in March; the Fosteriana, 9–16 in. (22–40 cm), early April; and the Greigii, 9–20 in. (22–50 cm), mid-April. The other divisions comprise early, mid-season, and late categories. The earlies begin blooming in mid-April; mid-seasons from the end of April; and lates from the beginning of May.

Earlies which flower in April comprise two divisions, singles and doubles, and range from 10 to 15 in. (25–37 cm).

Mid-season, flowering from late April, comprise the Mendels, Triumphs, and Darwin hybrids, and range from 15 in. to just over 2 ft (37–60 cm).

Lates which begin flowering in May include Darwins (not their hybrids), Lily-flowered, Rembrandt, Parrot, Cottage, and Double-Late, ranging up to 30 in. (75 cm).

Bulb catalogues list each class of tulip separately and clearly so that choosing is easy. To make it even easier, the catalogues also offer collections of each class. Planting should be done in late autumn and early winter in good soil and preferably a sunny situation. Planted bulbs should be covered with 3 inches (7 cm) of soil.

Generally all bulbs to bloom in summer (June onwards) are planted in spring. Those to bloom in late winter, spring, and early summer are planted from late September onwards. Except when following my hints for planting the lawn, daffodils benefit from early planting. A rough general guide to depth of planting is that a bulb should have twice its own depth of soil on top of it. This means that a bulb 1 inch (2·5 cm) in diameter wants 2 inches (5 cm) of soil above it, so the hole must be 3 inches (7 cm) deep. Here are some bulbous subjects worth a place in every garden.

WINTER- AND SPRING-FLOWERING BULBS

Bluebell. 12 in. (30 cm). A humble thing, not found in all catalogues. May be listed as Endymion. Flowers blue, pink, or white. Blooms in May. Excellent under trees.

Chionodoxa (Glory-of-the-Snow). 6 in. (15 cm), Blue, white, or pink. March–April. Suitable for growing in the front of borders or in grass, and also useful in the rock garden (rock gardening is dealt with in Chapter 11).

Crocus chrysanthus. A corm. 3–4 in. (7–10 cm). White, yellow, blue, mauve, and other shades. January–March. Prefers sunny site but not fussy. Dislikes heavy rain when in bloom.

Erythronium dens-canis (Dog's tooth violet). 4–6 in. (10–15 cm). White and shades of yellow, orange, and pink. March–April. Once planted are best left undisturbed for several years.

Iris Reticulata. 6 in. (15 cm). Violet-purple. February–March. Good for the rockery. Very hardy and will bloom amid snow and ice in a bleak winter.

Muscari (Grape Hyacinth). 4–8 in. (10–20 cm). Blue or white. April–May. Congested clumps should be lifted and divided in autumn and replanted immediately.

Narcissi. Up to 2 ft (60 cm). Those with big trumpets are the daffodils, while the remainder are known simply as narcissi. Yellow, pink, white, with some orange. March–May.

Snowdrops. 6–8 in. (15–20 cm). May be listed in your catalogues under their botanical name of Galanthus. White with green markings. January–March. Can be naturalized. Plant close together in small clumps.

Tulips. 12–30 in. (30–75 cm). A wide range with a good choice of colourings. Blooms from mid-April onwards as described earlier in this chapter.

SUMMER FLOWERING

Acidanthera murielae. 3 ft (1 m). August. White. Scented. Somewhat similar to gladioli. Not truly hardy but given a sheltered spot beside a warm wall they will bloom. Also can be grown indoors.

Chincherinchees (Onrithogalum thyrsoides). 18–24 in. (45–60 cm). August. Packed spikes of ivory-white flowers. Very long-lasting as cut flowers.

Crocosmia masonorum, a hardy corm. 2 ft (60 cm). Orange-red. July. This is like a high-quality montbretia. Its arching flower-stems have short spikes of trumpety flowers.

Dahlia. Various heights, shapes, and colours. Late summer to autumn. Following is a selection of dahlias, all of which are reasonably easy to grow, if dealt with as suggested earlier in this chapter. The 'decorative' dahlias are those with broad petals.

Miniature-flowered Decorative: Lilianne Ballego, bronze; Kochelsee, bright red; Musetts, red and white.

Small-flowered Decorative: Gerrie Hoek, deep pink; Glory of Heemstede, primrose-yellow; Chinese Lantern, orange-red with yellow background.

Medium-flowered Decorative: Deuil du Roi Albert, purple with white tips; Majuba, deep red; Snow Country, white.

Small-flowered Cactus: Doris Day, cardinal-red; Purple Gem, cyclamen; Preference, pink.

Medium-flowered Cactus: Apple Blossom, pink; Hoek's Glory, lavender.

Galtonia candicans, also known as 'Hyacinthus candicans'. 3–4 ft (1–1·25 m). White. July–September. Its tall spikes of lightly scented flowers make an attractive display.

Gladiolus. Various heights and colours. Flowering all summer. The following are fairly easy to grow.

Earlies – Green Woodpecker: an unusual colour. Greenish yellow with red in the throat. Useful in flower arrangements. Life Flame: a bright flame-scarlet. Pendion: rosy lavender with blotches of violet.

Mid-season – D'Artagnan: a striking bloom in creamy white with heavy blotching of cherry-scarlet. Flowersong: favoured by show growers. Golden yellow. Oscar: deep crimson-scarlet.

Lates – New Europe: geranium-red Aristocrat: purplish red with lighter edge. Bloemfontein: salmon, blotched yellow.

Lily. 2–6 ft (60 cm–2 m). Various colours. Flowering most of the summer. Some species and hybrid lilies follow:

Species Lilies

Lilium Auratum. 4–5 ft (1·25–1·5 m), blooms August–September. This is the Golden-rayed Lily of Japan, with large open, white flowers, several to a stem. A gold ray runs down the centre of each petal. Strongly scented. Some people call it the Queen of the Lilies.

Lilium Henryi. 5–6 ft (1·5–2 m). August. Orange-yellow reflexed flowers up to thirty on a stem.

Gladioli (Green Spot, Bon Voyage, Pandion, Life Flame, Mr. W. Cobley)

Gladoli Butterfly Mixed

Lilium Martagon. 4 ft (1·25 m). June–July. Flowers vary from light purple to pale purplish pink. Called the Turk's Cap Lily because of the shape of the hanging reflexed blooms.

Lilium Regale. 3–4 ft (1–1·25 m). July. Flowers large, funnel-shaped, white inside with yellow in the throat, and wine-red markings outside. Probably the best known of all the lilies. Heavily scented and easy to grow.

Lilium speciosum maelpomene. 5–6 ft (1·5–2 m). August. Pinkish-white rolled-back petals, heavily spotted purplish red.

Lilium Tigrinum Splendens. 4–5 ft (1·25–1·5 m). August–September. Orange-red flowers spotted with glossy black. The best of the Tiger Lilies.

(All except Martagon are stem-rooting.)

Hybrid Lilies

Citronella Strain. 3–4 ft (1–1·25 m). July. Yellow recurved pendant blooms, up to thirty on a stem, spotted black.

Enchantment. 3 ft (1 m). June. Nasturtium-red, upright cup-shaped blooms, up to sixteen on a stem.

Fire King. 3 ft (1 m). July. Orange-red outward-facing blooms with purple spotting.

Royal Gold. 4 ft (1·25 m). July. Golden-yellow trumpets, like a coloured version of the Regal Lily.

The last of these four is a Trumpet Hybrid in the Chinese group. The three others are Asiatic Hybrids. (They are stem-rooters, except for Citronella.)

Leucojum aestivum, the summer snowflake. 1½ ft (45 cm). White. April–May. Has strap-shaped leaves, above which rise the flower-spikes carrying inch-long flowers whose white petals have green tips.

Montbretia. 2 ft (60 cm). Yellow and orange shades. July–September. These need a sheltered spot if grown in cold districts. Sword-shaped leaves and arching flower-stems. Buy in April–May and plant promptly as they dislike being out of the ground.

Ranunculus aconitifolius (Fair Maids of France). 2 ft (60 cm). White. May and June. Related to the common buttercup. The double-flowered Flore-pleno is most popular. It has shiny petals and thrives in sun or half shade.

Amaryllis

Begonia

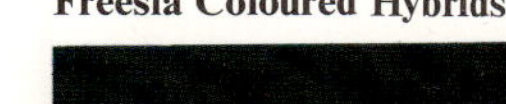

Freesia Coloured Hybrids

8 Roses

Rose-growing doubtless has problems. Roses can be difficult for people of limited experience and they demand such attention at times as might put them outside the range of easy plants, but there are three important points to make. One is that there are easy ways, if it is accepted that perfection is not mandatory. Another is that no garden should ignore a truly popular subject. The third is that one can grow two or three specimens without running into the problems that arise when they are grown on a larger scale. I realize that people who start off doing something on a small scale sometimes find that the bug gets them and they become keen. I must try, therefore, to give these subjects reasonable treatment while pointing out short-cuts and ways of achieving acceptable results without strenuous or time-consuming effort.

The problem which causes most confusion is pruning. First of all, the approach to it is often wrong. There is an impression that pruning requires some magic touch which if properly applied will make a scraggy little rose bush produce blooms capable of winning top prizes in shows. This comes from reading intricate details of how to make the right cuts in the right places at the right time. Or people get ideas from watching a skilled operator at work. When a specialist writes about rose-pruning he is expecting to help the *enthusiast* increase his skill. All this tricky guidance is sixth-form stuff, and if you are a first-former you need not try to understand it fully. Furthermore, if you have no ambition to reach sixth-form standards you can stick to more elementary methods. Begin by looking at the basic reason for pruning – not the sophisticated aims of those who practise higher techniques. A rose bush left untrimmed tends to go tall and straggly. Some shoots may be damaged in various ways and some may become diseased. If no trimming (pruning) is done, lengthening growths will become bare except at the top, then new shoots will spring from low down and will rob the top-growth so that it weakens and dies.

So the first aim must be to keep the size of the bush down to reasonable proportions, and to shorten shoots which are beginning to go bare for a great part of their length. That is the exercise, and it may sound complicated. But there is nothing complicated about the answer. I advise for the beginner a simple general rule, which is to cut out half of the year's growth on every shoot. In addition you must obviously remove any shoots which look unhealthy (shedding their leaves too soon and so on) and any that are criss-crossing. The first advance on that simple rule is to learn how to treat strong, vigorous-growing plants differently from the way you treat weak-growing specimens. Here you need to learn to do the opposite of what some people's logic might make them want to do. You might be tempted to think that the strong and vigorous can stand severe cutting but that the weak cannot. But the correct treatment goes the opposite way. The weak need cutting back severely in the hope that such treatment will stimulate new and stronger growth. The vigorous must be allowed to follow their natural characteristic of showing strength

(above left) Rose bush before pruning

(above right) Rose bush shown in previous picture has now been pruned.

(right) Pruning cuts must be made cleanly, with sharp tools, and at a gentle angle. The cut should go from a ¼ inch (6 mm) above the bud to just level with it on the opposite side of the stem.

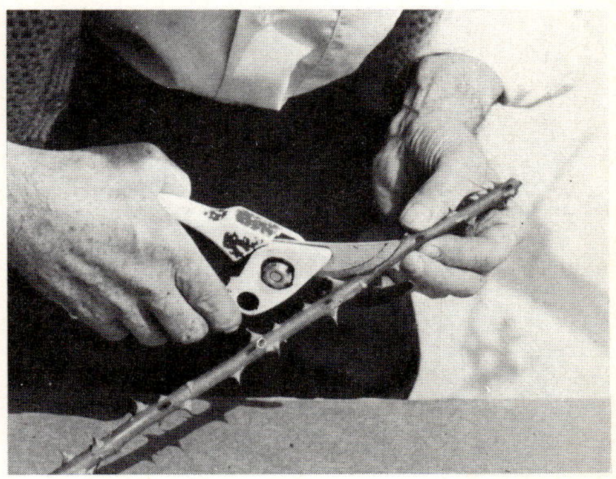

and vigour. You can't convert them into dwarfs. Although roses vary in habit, the variations make the pruning needs fairly obvious. Generally, you will find that floribunda types (those with mop-heads of blooms) are more vigorous than the hybrid-tea types (those with not so many blooms to a stem). The floribundas therefore must be allowed to grow taller. There are other types known as 'shrub roses', which are taller still (5 feet – 1·5 m – and upwards).

Roses which climb or are trained against walls or on posts and pillars are different. Some, which bloom only on year-old wood, should have the flowering stems cut out after flowering. Others need varying degrees of pruning. If you grow any of these, you should ask the nurseryman what method of pruning to adopt. The complications hardly qualify for full explanation in a book on easy gardening. One rose-pruning exercise which is often misunderstood concerns the class of rose known as the 'climbing sport'. This is a popular and growing class produced by a mutation called 'sporting' in which a bush-type rose changes its character and takes on the same habit of growth as a climbing rose. You can identify these 'sports' in your catalogues by their names, because they retain the name of the bush variety from which they sprang plus the prefix 'Climbing'. Thus, if you get a climber that has sported from the Hybrid-tea bush rose called Ena Harkness, the climber will be named 'Climbing Ena Harkness'. These climbing sports retain one characteristic of the bush type from which they sprang, that is, they tend to make their best, if not all, blooms towards the tips of their shoots. If you encourage them to spurt upwards you might easily have 12- or 15-foot (4 or 5 m) stems, bare all the way except for a foot or so at the tip and out of reach. The correct way to grow these climbing sports is to train their main stems as near the horizontal as possible. You will need to use supports and to tie the stems in the outstretched positions. The effect of this training is that side-shoots appear along the main stems and the side-shoots carry flowers. Climbing Peace, like its bush-type parent, is very vigorous and I have to turn some of its side-shoots horizontally, the same as the main stems, because they grow far too long. Flowering shoots then spring from the bent-down side-shoots.

When to prune is a matter of controversy, but the casual gardener need not get involved in the argument. The chief controversy concerns people who want blooms at the right date for a show, and people who want a well-timed display from a fair number of plants. Timing is based on the fact that a plant takes a certain number of weeks to produce a flower from a shoot stimulated by a pruning cut made in spring. The period is not precise because weather variations can shorten or lengthen it. The other controversy concerns whether it is better to prune in early winter or wait till spring. One of the arguments in favour of winter pruning is that the plant will 'grow with the weather', meaning that the pruning will not stimulate a sudden rush of growth. Sudden growth can be tender and may be nipped by a sudden spell of sharp frost. One of the arguments in favour of spring pruning is that with the sap running, the pruning cut heals up quickly and is not susceptible to diseases which may be floating around in the air. I favour a slight compromise. I like to trim off heavy top-growth on tall plants in winter so that the plants do not rock in the wind and so that some bits of disease and some pests can be disposed of right away. The main pruning, to get plants properly shaped and sized, is done any time I find convenient from February onwards. A showman would probably do his pruning in mid-March.

Those of you who inherit roses when taking over a garden need to regenerate plants which have been allowed to get too woody. Tackle the problem on lines similar to those suggested earlier in this chapter for dealing with plants which have begun to get too tall. In other words, don't try to correct the trouble at one go but rather eliminate the hard old wood gradually over a period of about three years.

(left) Dearest
(below) All Gold
(right) Orange Sensation

Evelyn Fison

Keen types make preparation of the ground sound like a great deal of hard graft. Whether all the double digging and other off-putting chores do any good for rose showmen, I do not know. I don't indulge in such extravagant exercise and my roses have never complained. If your ground needs double digging it must be in a bad way, and all you will grow on it is tired. It is definitely worth while digging the ground to a spade's depth and this is not hard work if you remember to stand with both feet close up to the spade and do not lean forward at any time during the operation. It is also worth while pushing a fork into the ground immediately below the spade's depth and giving it a wriggle or two to loosen the lower strata of soil. You can scatter a general fertilizer on the ground and let the rain wash it in. This digging exercise should be completed a month ahead of planting if possible, so that the ground can settle just a little and the fertilizer can get washed in. So you can do this preparation in October for November planting – or later for late planting – and you can plant right up to March. But never worry if you need to dig and plant all at one go.

Improving the soil as you dig is always a good thing. This does not mean working in loads of farmyard muck, even if you can get it. For one thing, roses do better in the first year after planting if the soil is not too rich but just moderately well fed. For another, their roots don't like contact with strong manure, any more than do other plant roots. But, not least important, heavy doses of fertilizer either wash away and are wasted, or they can make the plant sick if the roots absorb too much of it. Believe me, I am not poking fun at those enthusiastic rose-growers who spare neither sweat nor cash in trying to make the soil as rich and sweet as they can make it. If any of them reads this, let him be reminded that this chapter is not for rose specialists but for people who want to limit the time and labour they put into the garden and who do not want to win show prizes.

After preparation, comes the planting. For labour saving I suggest that you do not devote a whole bed to four or five dozen rose plants. Rather you should slot them in, three or six in a group, among the other plants in your borders. In some ways it is admittedly easier to look after roses in a large batch. In fact I find it so with the large number which I have growing in rows. They have been sent to me for testing and it is easier to keep an eye on them when they are regimented. These make a convenient pattern for such routine treatments as feeding, weeding, and spraying. The disadvantage of having a large batch is that any sort of neglect becomes clearly noticeable; whereas small groups dotted around among other plants do not make their faults so obvious. That is why I think the leisurely approach suggests this method rather than large groupings. When you buy your roses in containers, it is easy to position them precisely where you want them to grow. You just take the plants in their pots and stand them in place, shuffling them around as necessary until you are fully satisfied. A little pressure on the container will then make an indent in the soil to mark the position so that you can scoop out a hole and place the plant in it. But even with the older method – buying dormant plants – there is no difficulty in positioning roses accurately. You begin by sticking a short cane into the ground to mark each place where you want a rose to grow.

Unlike the procedure with some plantings, where the marker cane gets in the way of the plant, the cane for a rose can stay where it is, and the rose can be planted right up to it. This is because the nurseryman's method of rose propagation produces a plant with a one-sided root system. If you place the palm of your hand flat on the ground and hold your forearm vertical, you can imagine your arm as the rose stem and your spread fingers as the roots – all on one side of the stem. This is quite different from some subjects, such as a young apple tree, where the root system covers a full circle round the base of the stem.

I have explained this so that you can see what I mean about how easy it is to give your roses the precise positioning you aim at. You dig a shallow hole at one side of the cane (instead of all round it) and you rest the stem of the rose bush against the cane, with the roots spread in the hole. Make sure you do really *spread* those roots. For convenience of packing, the roots may be hanging downwards when you get them, like a hand hanging from a wrist. But you should gently bend them till they are nearly at right angles to the stem. This automatically aids shallow planting, which is desired. By the time your rose bush settles in, it should be sitting at the same depth as it was in the nursery. To achieve this you plant it so that the soil-level is about an inch above the old planting-mark (clearly visible as a soil-mark on the stem) and the depth will be just right when the soil has settled.

A bucket of peat or fine soil with a sprinkling of bonemeal stirred into it is a great help at planting time. Work a little of this into the soil close to the roots and it will encourage production of the very fine feeding roots which have to grow from the thick fleshy root system. The soil should be trodden fairly firmly round the roots after planting to remove air pockets. One little trick here is to begin the treading according to whether the plant seems to be sitting at the height you want it or not. If it seems to be sitting too low, tread first all round the outside of the planting hole and you will find that the middle will rise a little, lifting the plant with it. If the plant is sitting a fraction high, tread first with your feet as close to the plant as you can get. This will press down the middle of the hole and lower the plant at the same time. After treading, ruffle the soil with your finger-ends to discourage caking, because caking blocks the much-needed air flow.

Most roses are grown as bushes in small or large groups, in beds or borders. At one time the choice was simpler because we had only hybrid teas (large-flowered, and mostly grown one to a stem) and polyantha (cluster-flowered). The polyanthas were grown chiefly for bedding or decoration rather than for cutting or for button-holes. Over the years, new breeding and much inter-breeding has caused us to change the naming of classes and to create new classes. Instead of hybrid teas we refer now to hybrid-tea types. Besides the polyantha (which are still around and still sweet) we have floribunda. These are cluster-flowered but their flowers are much larger. More recently, we have increased the sizes of individual blooms in the clusters of some of the floribundas and these are now referred to as hybrid-tea-type floribundas. Some growers call them 'grandifloras'. I explain this not to pack your head with baffling detail but, on the contrary, to warn you to be prepared for such detail and not to take much notice of it. For your border rose, you can choose either hybrid-tea types, which do not have a mass of blooms on each stem, or floribunda types which have mop-heads of bloom. For the subdivisions that come after that you need concern yourself only with the heights the varieties reach. For example, some hybrid-tea-type floribundas grow too tall to associate with other types, so you should avoid bad mixing. But really, the casual or busy gardener does not need to do his own precise choosing. The nurseryman offers attractive collections and the individual varieties in each collection have been selected with care to make sure that they will look good as a group.

I would go further, and say that many people who have grown roses for years have not yet mastered them well enough to choose wisely from a big and bewildering

Wendy Cussons

Super Star

Ernest H. Morse

catalogue. They would do better if they bought a collection as chosen by the grower, instead of making individual choices. If you want to do a bit of choosing for yourself here are some I would suggest for your consideration.

Floribundas with strong fragrance:

Arthur Bell, yellow
Dearest, rosy salmon
Elizabeth of Glamis, light salmon
Escapade, magenta with white reverse
Orange Sensation, light vermilion

Other good floribundas:

Allgold, golden yellow
Dorothy Wheatcroft, brilliant red
Evelyn Fison, vivid red with scarlet
Iceberg, white
Queen Elizabeth, pink

Hybrid-tea types with strong fragrance:

Alec's Red, cherry-red
Bonsoir, peach-pink
Ernest H. Morse, turkey-red
Fragrant Cloud, geranium-red
John Waterer, deep red
Mala Rubenstein, pink
Mullard Jubilee, cerise-pink
Red Devil, scarlet
Super Star, light vermilion
Wendy Cussons, cerise with scarlet flush

Although roses should not have over-rich soil during their first season, I believe in giving a summer feed with a recognized rose fertilizer at the rate prescribed on the bag, as soon as the first summer flush begins to fade – say mid-July.

Weeds are inevitable among roses as among most other subjects which do not smother the soil. But this creates no problem with modern techniques unless you wait too long and let the weeds get tall. The technique is to knock down the weeds with a herbicide such as Weedol. This does not always kill them completely. Some of them will regrow because their roots are not killed. But you cannot have a herbicide which is safe to use among plants, and at the same time expect it to be a complete and final knock-out. Two or three applications a season may be needed. To apply this herbicide effectively and effortlessly you need what is termed a Weedol Applicator (what a pity people cannot think of shorter and more attractive words!). This appli-

Elizabeth of Glamis

Iceberg

cator is a gallon flask with anti-splash, screw-on cap and a long tube, instead of the spout you get on a watering-can. Also, instead of the rose-end which you would find on the spout, the applicator has a slim perforated tube called a 'dribble-bar'. There are different lengths of dribble-bar including very short ones to allow manœuvring round rose bushes without splashing. (*See* Chapter 18 on tools.)

To keep down labour here, it is wise to catch the weeds before they reach into the branches of the bushes. If they do get tall, a good sharp hoe is an easy and effective tool for coping with them. The easy way with roses is rather ruthless and the expert way is time-consuming. I compromise between the two, but must admit that with years of experience behind me I can do a great deal without using up much time or effort. Still, the principle of easy going is there, and for the plants it boils down to something approaching the survival of the fittest. My roses get a certain amount of routine help to keep them fit and happy. Those which do not respond would at one time have gone into my sick bay so that I could nurse them back to health. Now I have no time for this fussing so the failures are written off. For leisurely gardening this is the most practical approach. The alternative is to give more time to a weakling than to the whole of the remainder. Tending to the weak at the expense of the strong is always my way with humans and animals, but not with plants. I believe that by eliminating weakling plants I end up with a gardenful of healthy plants. The weakling may be diseased and if you keep the plant the disease may spread.

From other people's experience, I learn sometimes that an attractive variety which I have thrown out as a failure must have been merely the victim of a chance infection. In that event I may try replacing it. But that is an exception. What I have described is far removed from neglect. To be really negligent is to give no plant a proper chance. If pests and diseases are neglected they can spread through the whole stock of roses. So one must be on the look-out and take precautions. (*See* Chapter 17.)

9 Flowers from Seed

Broadly speaking, an annual is a plant which completes its life cycle in one year, beginning from seed, growing to maturity, flowering, making its fruit (or seed), and then dying. A biennial starting from seed will make a mature plant one year, then take a rest, and later reawaken to produce its flowers and seeds the next year. I use the term 'broadly speaking' because gardeners can get up to such tricks as sowing annuals one year to flower the next, or persuading biennials to flower in the same season as they are sown. The vegetable garden contains many biennials which we never treat as such. For instance, cabbages, carrots, turnips, and a whole range of plants of which we eat the roots or leaves, are not allowed to complete their two-year life cycle. Indeed if a plant in one of these categories hurries into flower in its first season we complain that it has 'gone to seed'. I mention this because we need to learn how to avoid that 'going to seed'. Annuals and biennials are in three classes which we term 'hardy', 'half-hardy', and 'tender'. But let us move on from definitions and characteristics, and consider what part annual and biennial flowers can play in helping the gardener who wants to achieve all he can with the minimum expenditure of time and effort.

Consider first the hardy annuals. Their so-called 'hardiness' means that they need no protection, but can be sown direct into the open ground just where they are wanted to flower. This does not bar them from other treatment, such as early sowing under glass to give them an extended season. The range is tremendous, covering every shape, size, colour, and height, as you can see from the catalogues which pop through your letter-boxes in the New Year. These are catalogues which I do advise you to explore and to use adventurously. People are inclined to stick to the items they know extremely well and to ignore the many new ones which come into the catalogues each year as the result of patient scientific work by plant-breeders. My advice is to take a fair proportion of what you are sure about, but add a few subjects which are either quite new or are new to you. You will see here that I am referring to your seed order rather than to plant-buying. That is because the commercial grower of annual flowering plants cannot risk being too adventurous. He is fully conscious of the point I have made, that people are conservative in their choice. Therefore if he tries to push too many new ideas he will probably have the plants left on his hands. His profit margins are too small for him to take that risk.

This brings us to the need for sowing some of our own. Looking at the wide range of hardy annuals, the secrets of success from seed are few and simple. Seed wants a soil that is reasonably fine and crumbly – fine so that the seed snuggles in and feels secure rather than being suspended among a few soil lumps, and crumbly so that there is room for that essential movement of moisture and air among the fine particles. Seeds in general do not want to be buried, but merely covered lightly with little more than their own thickness of soil. They should not be overcrowded but some of the fine ones do much better when near enough together to make a joint effort at pushing the soil off them as their shoots seek the light. The best

(top) Cornflower, Polka Dot Mixed (HA)
(above) Poppy, Pink Chiffon (HA)

seed packets usually give more than enough information to ensure success, and if everyone read those instructions carefully almost every seed would grow. Raising plants from seed has been made much easier by the introduction of pelleted seeds. These pellets are small pills of a carefully balanced mixture, each with a seed in the middle. Details of the pellets and how to use them will be found in the seed-sowing section of Chapter 16, entitled Propagation, which deals with all the common methods of plant raising. Let us just say that you would do well to choose seed in pelleted form where it is available.

If we consider first how to do the major effort, say sowing a whole border, we can adapt the technique to the smallest of areas – even down to barely a square foot (9 sq dm). The production of a small border of mixed annuals is the lazy man's delight and the flower-lover's dream picture. First of all, the preparation needed is not heavy, because annuals do not like a rich soil. Choose a spot that has a bright outlook, rather than a shady corner. Prick the soil surface with a garden fork, rake off the weeds, and sprinkle on a normal dressing of the general fertilizer you have bought for the rest of the garden. From that point, I like to allow a couple of weeks if possible for the fertilizer to wash in and for weed seeds near the surface to spring up and be removed.

Another light raking then will ensure that the fertilizer is thoroughly mixed into the soil. I then draw a series of straight lines with a stick or the corner of the rake to create little furrows called 'seed drills' all along the bed.

(below, left to right) Salvia Horminum (Clary) (HA); Silene, Dwarf Double Salmon (HA); Nigella, Persian Jewels (HA)

These are made about $\frac{1}{2}$ inch (13 mm) deep and a foot (30 cm) apart. Next, the furrowed border is treated as if it were a country map. A stick is used to draw lots of wiggly lines as if to divide the country into odd-shaped and odd-sized counties. Each 'county' should become the home of one subject, its seed being sown thinly in the furrows inside its county boundaries. Before any seed is sown I make a label for each subject and lay the label and its appropriate packet in its spot. A bit of shuffling goes on while I decide which is the best spot for each item. I do *not* approve of regimentation such as putting the tallest in the back row, the medium in the middle, and the shortest in front. What is important is that where a tall item is placed in the front row there should be other tall items just behind it, rather than small ones which would become hidden.

There may be people who would want to query two points in the procedure so far prescribed – feeding and the method of making the seed drills. On feeding, it is well known that overfed annual plants grown from seed make excessive leaf growth at the expense of flower production. But the normal dressing (as prescribed on the bag according to brand) is not an excessive amount of fertilizer. It will not make

Tropaeolum (Canary Creeper) (HA)

(below) Nasturtium, Jewel Mixed (HA)
(bottom left) Phacelia Campanularia (HA)
(bottom right) Calendula, Pacific Beauty (HA)

the soil rich. The anxiety to avoid giving annuals over-rich soil causes many people to starve them to the point where plants flower quickly enough but poorly, and they go to seed too soon.

You may feel that drawing straight furrows before dividing the border into irregular sections is an abandonment of the informality which is one of the big joys of a border of annuals. In theory, it may seem that these furrows will produce a regimented look, but not at all. The variations in shape and height of plants, and the irregular outlines of the individual groups eradicate regimentation. However thinly you sow, more plants will come up than you need, so you must pull out a few to give the remainder adequate room to grow and bloom.

Once the seed is placed in the drill, the soil should be knocked down from the sides of the drill to cover the seed lightly – never deeply – and the surface should be made firm by such action as tapping it down gently with the head of the rake. Do not scrub out the irregular lines which you drew to indicate the boundaries separating one subject from another.

The number of divisions need not correspond precisely to the number of packets of seed you are using. There is nothing to prevent you having two or more sections filled with the same subject, but keep them well apart and try to achieve reasonable colour blendings or good contrasts.

Sowing of hardy annuals outdoors is an operation where you might expect early timing to produce earlier results and a consequent longer season of bloom, but this does not always work if the soil is cold or unready. The ground should be crumbly and reasonably moist and the weather should not be too bleak. If I worked to the calendar I should say that mid-March was good average time with a week earlier in warm districts and a couple of weeks later in cold districts. But wherever you are, you will find that undue haste does not gain you anything over the patient neighbour who bides his time and waits till he judges conditions to be right. Nevertheless, the man in a hurry has to sow when he can find time, and accept what comes. Sowing can continue up to mid-April for hardy annuals. For half-hardy annuals, direct sowing outdoors should wait till May. The procedure is similar except that one tends to use bigger clumps of fewer subjects – perhaps a whole bed of one variety. The more popular method is to sow early – January onwards – under glass, for planting out later. This gives a longer flowering season.

Don't think that I am advocating a border of hardy annuals as a good example of an easy-work gardening feature. I have detailed the procedure for making such a border, large or small, partly because it is easy enough for those who grasp the idea, and also because it covers the points you need to know for making proper use of these wonderful, adaptable subjects in a simple way all over the garden in various small pockets. They are especially useful to close temporary gaps between shrubs (*see* Chapter 5) which have been planted far enough apart to allow them to make their full spread as they grow. If you get the drill right – a little feeding, thorough raking, thin sowing, and so on – you can employ annuals anywhere you like.

The general run of annuals, hardy or half-hardy, which you dot about the garden or in the hardy-annual border, should not be given formal staking unless they are tall. But sometimes they want a little support and it is wise to have some short twiggy sticks which you can thrust into their midst so that groups of plants grow among the twigs to find their own support. And they hide the twigs.

Annuals have a strong natural passion for ensuring the survival of the species.

Since they know they have only a short life, they produce seed prolifically as quickly as they can. Instinctively, they seem satisfied to die once they have produced that seed. So you can see that the way to keep them flowering freely over a long period is to frustrate them in their seed-producing efforts. To do this you either keep picking flowers, if you want them for home decoration, or snap off the flower-heads as soon as the petals fade, and before the seed-pods can swell.

There are plenty of gardeners who class the sweet pea as the queen of the hardy annuals. It certainly is a wonderful subject for ease of growth, freedom of flowering (including plenty for cutting), length of season, range of charming colours, and not least, scent. In an effort to do them justice, sweet peas are given a section to themselves at the end of this chapter.

Apart from the hardy and half-hardy annuals, there is another section – the more tender subjects which are easy to raise and cultivate in a greenhouse but not outdoors. They are dealt with in Chapter 15 on greenhouse gardening.

HARDY ANNUALS

Out of the hundreds of other hardy annuals I will try to name a few which will appeal to the casual and busy gardener.

Alyssum Dwarf Cushion. Excellent for edging or bedding. 3–6 in. (7–15 cm) tall. Variety Carpet of Snow, white, packed in pellet form. Other good varieties include Oriental Night, deep violet-purple; Little Dorrit, white; and Rosie O'Day, lilac-pink.

Anchusa capensis, Blue Bird. 15 in. (37 cm). Like a large forget-me-not with gentian-blue flowers. Some class it as half-hardy but I find it hardy.

Calendula, Pacific Beauty. 18 in.–2 ft (45–60 cm). This is the Pot Marigold, sometimes called the Scotch and sometimes the English Marigold.

Candytuft. Quick-growing in any soil or situation. Mixes well with alyssum. Variety Giant Hyacinth-flowered White. Stands 15 in. (37 cm) tall. Fairy Mixture (pelleted), in a range of bright colours, is 9 in. (22 cm) tall.

Clarkia Elegans, double. In delicate mixed colours, 2–2½ ft (60–75 cm). Pelleted seeds. In normal seed form are Clarkia pulchella, mixed colours. 1½–2 ft (45–60 cm).

Chrysanthemum (annual varieties). Not to be confused with the large family of border chrysanthemums. These annuals, in a lovely range of colours, mostly grow less than 2 ft (60 cm) tall, but a few grow taller.

Convolvulus, minor mixed. Little over 1 ft (30 cm) tall. Related to the well-known Morning Glory climber. Royal Ensign has lovely trumpet-shaped flowers of rich blue with white at the base and a yellow eye.

Cornflower Polka Dot. Dwarf mixture of several colours. 15–18 in. (37–45 cm). Pelleted seed available.

Cosmos, Goldilocks. 2–3 ft (60 cm–1 m) with star-like flowers in golden yellow, carried in long sprays, good for cutting. Foliage is fern-like and attractive.

Eschscholzia, the Californian Poppy. 12–15 in. (30–37 cm). The Harlequin Hybrids comprise many bright colours. A mixture of pastel shades is offered in pelleted form.

Godetia, Dwarf Bedding Mixed. 9–12 in. (22–30 cm). Compact plants with flowers in shades of pink, salmon, crimson, blotched, striped, and picotee-edged. Pellets available.

Larkspur. Long stems of delphinium-type flowers in shades of blue, scarlet,

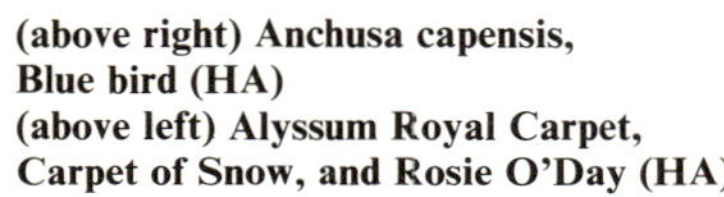

(above right) Anchusa capensis,
Blue bird (HA)
(above left) Alyssum Royal Carpet,
Carpet of Snow, and Rosie O'Day (HA)

(middle) Linum grandiflorum rubrum,
and album (HA)

(below left) Larkspur, Tall Branching (HA)
(below right) Godetia, Dwarf Mixed (HA)

Eschscholzia, Ballerina (HA)

Linaria, Fairy Bouquet (HA)

Chrysanthemum Annual (HA)

Cosmos diversifolius (HA) – Goldilocks

lilac, salmon, and white. Growing over 3 ft (1 m) tall.

Lavatera Tanagra. 3½–4 ft (1–1·25 m). Free-flowering bushy plants with blooms 3–4 in. in diameter in shining, deep cerise-pink.

Linaria, Fairy Bouquet. 9 in. (22 cm). A dwarf compact plant with large blooms in a mixture of many bright colours. Pellets available.

Linum Grandiflorum album. Graceful plant up to 2 ft (60 cm) tall with crimson-centred white flowers.

Matthiola bicornis (Night-scented Stock). 1 ft (30 cm) tall with lilac-mauve flowers whose chief quality is the amazing fragrance they put out at dusk. Grow them near a doorway or open window where the scent will not be wasted.

Mignonette. Less than 1 ft (30 cm) tall but another bundle of wonderful fragrance. Flowers are insignificant.

Nasturtium. Inclined to trail and cover a good deal of space, plants smothering themselves with bloom. The Dwarf Jewel Mixture holds its flowers, of many shades, well above the foliage.

Nigella (Love-in-a-Mist), Miss Jekyll. Grows 15 in. (37 cm) tall with sky-blue flowers. Also Persian Jewels – a colourful mixture.

Phacelia, Blue Bonnet. Grows up to about 18 in. (45 cm) with deep blue flowers. Also Campanularia, 9 in. (22 cm).

Poppy, Pink Chiffon. Paeony-type, double flowers of bright pink on 2-ft (60 cm) stems. Free-blooming, and happy in almost any soil.

Salvia Horminum (Clary). 1½ ft (45 cm). The highly coloured bracts (modified leaves) are attractive in flower arrangements. Varieties Blue Bird and Pink Cloud are coloured as named, while variety Colour Blend is a mixture of bright pink, violet-blue, and white.

Sunflower, Autumn Sunshine. Medium-sized flowers in lovely colour combinations, mixing bronzes, reds, and yellows and carried on stems about 4 ft (1·25 m) tall.

Silene. Dwarf cushion flower, popular in rockeries but useful also as an edging plant. Comes in various colour mixtures.

Tropaeolum Canariensis (Canary Creeper). An easy-going climber with pale green foliage and yellow flowers, nicely fringed.

Virginian Stock. 9 in. (22 cm). Has been one of the best-known and most popular little plants for several generations. Variety Crimson King is a rosy crimson. A mixture is also available.

Sweet Peas

There are several types of sweet pea and all are popular, but perhaps the most exciting of modern introductions is the new hedge type known as Jet-Set. Its varieties all grow about 3 feet (1 m) tall, similar to an older type known as Knee-Hi, and some of them have proved outstanding prizewinners. One Jet-Set variety, Madrid (bright scarlet) won a Bronze Medal in the 1974 All-Britain Trials, and an R.H.S. First-Class Certificate in 1972. Westminster (crimson), and Naples (mid-blue), also won R.H.S. First-Class Certificates in 1972. The reason I give priority to Jet-Set is that its blooms give you all the good points of older types but being short, it needs no elaborate support and so will appeal to the busy gardener. The plants are sturdy, easy growers with flower-stems as big and strong as those of the tall types and with four to five well-placed, large blooms to a stem. Best choice for general garden purposes is the mixed packet whose seeds produce blooms of strong colours in blue, lavender, crimson, salmon, pink, and white.

If Jet-Set is the latest type, the Spencers certainly offer the biggest range of varieties. The Spencers are old-established climbers which up to some years ago used to produce all the show-winning blooms. Then the Galaxies stepped in. These are another class of climber, and carry more blooms to a stem (five to seven, compared with fours and the occasional five). A further type is Bijou, whose plants are just over a foot tall. They are excellent for window-boxes and can also be planted in beds and borders.

There are variations in methods of raising sweet peas from seed. They can be sown direct outdoors, where you want them to bloom. Perhaps the most popular time for such sowing is March onwards according to weather. I always sow 3 inches (7 cm) apart to allow for misses. Sowings at this time can be protected by cloches or it can be done in a garden-frame, in pots or boxes for later transplanting. The aim is merely to get a quicker start and not to coddle the plants with heat. Another method I like is to sow outdoors in September or October, using frames or cloches, but still doing no coddling. The elements they need protection from are excessive rain and wind, not the cold. They may make long growth during the autumn and winter, so they would need pinching out a few times to keep them dwarf. When doing autumn sowing, I sow three seeds to a 3-inch (7 cm) pot, ending up by retaining only the strongest of the three. The pots are plunged to the brim in the open ground and then covered with cloches, but the cloches are kept fully ventilated. Planted out into flowering positions is done in late February or March. The advantage of autumn sowing is that the plants flower much earlier. The outer skin of sweet peas can become hard and to help it split the seed is sometimes soaked overnight. Another trick to help it along is to nick the outer skin very carefully with a razor-blade on the side opposite the 'eye' from which the seedling shoot will burst.

When planting out, one must consider what support is needed for tall types. Many people prefer to get the supports firmly fixed before planting or sowing. Jet-Set and Knee-Hi will grow without supports, unless the situation is exposed, but it is better to give them a little support, either with twiggy sticks or with netting tied to canes. The tall-growing varieties definitely need support and this is best provided by netting held on long canes. I like to plant down both sides of the netting, putting the plants 9 inches (22 cm) apart and staggered. Staggered means that the plants along one side of the netting sit opposite the gaps between those on the other side. Most specialists advise spacing the plants a foot apart but I prefer the closer planting, unless the plants are very well fed and cared for by keen growers.

One point on which sweet peas differ from the general rule on annuals is that they *do* like rich soil. Enrich the ground deeply with compost, farmyard manure, or other material. Give extra plant food as soon as the flowers begin to show. Allow for the fact that sweet peas put on a great deal of growth and have vigorous root systems. Hence the extra feeding will not make them coarse or too leafy.

Jet-Set varieties are Killarney, salmon-pink on cream; Madrid, large bright scarlet; Naples, wavy mid-blue; Riviera, frilly rosy-lavender; Westminster, wavy crimson; or you can get a mixture.

In Galaxies, a good selection would be Blue Argo, mid-blue; Cream Whiz, cream; Eskimo, ruffled pure white; Great Scott, frilled salmon-rose; Lavender

Mesembryanthemum Criniflorum (HHA)

Sweet Peas, Mixed (HA)

Delight, mid-lavender; Rosie, frilled rose on cream ground; Scarlet Whiz, ruffled scarlet; Tangerine, rich orange-red; or you can buy Galaxy Mixed.

The Knee-Hi and Bijou are both offered in packets of mixed colours.

Among the tall Spencer varieties, I suggest such favourites as: Air Warden, orange-scarlet; Elizabeth Taylor, mauve; Geranium Pink Improved, cerise-red; Margot, cream; Mrs R. Bolton, pink; Stylish, mid-blue; Superfine, salmon-pink; White Ensign, white; Tell Tale, picotee-edged, white with pink border.

Antirrhinum Bright Butterflies (HHA)

Zinnia, Thumbelina (HHA)

Marigold, Dwarf French, Colour Magic (HHA)

Nemesia, Carnival (HHA)

The half-hardies can do most of the jobs which the hardies do, except that they need a warmer start. This means either a later start outdoors or sowing indoors. Their lists include many attractive items which are used in various ways – for brightening up the summer display, either by filling up dull, bare patches or by planting in tubs and window-boxes. The busy gardener need not plant them in quantity or in formal groupings but he will find good uses for a selection of them.

Sometimes plants are listed in catalogues as half-hardy annuals when botanically they are perennial. This is a sensible arrangement because the subjects concerned are best treated as half-hardy annuals and grown for one year only. A good example is antirrhinum, which you might know as Snapdragon. In mentioning antirrhinums let me call attention to the fact that the breeders have produced an extraordinarily wide choice of types, and a colour range as wide as the rainbow. Many of them are F1 Hybrids (the significance of which is explained in Chapter 16 on propagation). Most are used a great deal for the sort of mass planting which we call 'bedding', but do not be put off by any so described, even if you are determined to cut out bedding, because all such plants are equally useful in small groups. Perhaps the most outstanding bedding group is the F1 Hybrid Coronette growing 2 ft (60 cm) tall in a big selection of colours. Then there are the tall F1 Hybrid varieties ranging from 2 ft to 3 ft (60 cm–1 m) and the Double F1 Hybrids of about the same size. There are other intermediate and dwarf classes including the Tom Thumb varieties. In the general half-hardy list which follows I have selected some antirrhinum novelties which I am sure you will like.

Some perennials also can be treated as half-hardy annuals. Pansies, for instance, sown in spring will flower the same year.

The casual gardener is not compelled to raise his half-hardy annual plants by the popular method. The easiest drill of all is to buy plants in late May or early June. They are on sale in every town or village in hardware shops, seed shops, multiple stores, garden centres, and in the market place. However I have never accepted that the only alternative to black is white or that the alternative to best must be worst. If the best method (starting the seed indoors) in March or April is too much work for anyone wishing to produce a fair range of half-hardy plants, there is no reason why he should not try just one box that way, and sow the others the easier way – in the open ground in May. Or if sowing by any method is too much, one can compromise by sowing just a few seeds, while buying plants to satisfy remaining needs.

You would need to be totally disinterested in gardening to think of dispensing with half-hardy annual flowers completely. They are a delightful and colourful tribe. And if you have even just a slight interest, I should like you to realise that raising plants for yourself is good fun and gives an extra thrill on top of the enjoyment you get out of seeing them bloom in the garden. So while you keep your gardening as effortless as you can, do not write off every little task as too much effort, until you have at least made a small trial.

Ageratum, Blue Heaven. 8 in. (20 cm). Makes a lovely cushion of lavender-blue about 1 ft (30 cm) in diameter. Mixes well with many other dwarf subjects.

Antirrhinum. The Tom Thumb variety Magic Carpet is in an attractive colour range. Only 6 in. (15 cm) tall. Two F1 Hybrids in pelleted seed are Orange Pixie, 8–12 in. (20–30 cm), with orange-cerise butterfly-type flowers; and Sweetheart, 1 ft (30 cm), azalea-like flowers in a good colour mixture.

Arctotis Harlequin (African Daisy). 12–15 in. (30–37 cm). Elegant large daisy-like blooms in red, orange, yellow, apricot, cream, and white. Loves a sunny position.

Aster, Ostrich Plume mixture. 2 ft (60 cm). The very large flowers show a wide colour range with shades of violet, lavender, red and pink, and also white. All are good for cutting. Pelleted seed.

Begonia. 6–12 in. (15–30 cm). The fibrous-rooted, as distinct from corms, are perennials treated as annuals. A wonderful colour range. Some varieties have shiny bronze foliage. If sown under glass in January–February, and planted out in June, will bloom till frosted.

Helichrysum, Monstrosum double mixed. 2½ ft (75 cm). Everlasting flowers, suitable for drying, in rose, crimson, orange, yellow, and white.

Kochia (Burning Bush). 2 ft (60 cm). Not a flowering plant, but a lovely bush of pale green. Dot one or two at strategic points to give contrast. The foliage takes on scarlet and bronze colourings in the autumn.

Lobelia, Sapphire. 10 in. (25 cm). Deep blue small flowers with white eyes. Useful trailer for window-boxes and hanging-baskets, though it will live happily elsewhere. Bedding varieties such as Cambridge Blue and the mauve Rosamund are only 6 in. (15 cm) tall.

Marigold, African, Golden Age. 10 in. (25 cm). The French and African marigolds have been inter-bred so much that it is sometimes difficult to sort them out. This African is a neat, dwarf variety with broad-petalled, 3-in. (7 cm) flowers.

Marigold, Dwarf French, Colour Magic. 9 in. (22 cm). The flowers are a mixture of mahogany red, orange, and yellow. Makes a compact plant, free-flowering and near enough weather-proof.

Marigold, Dwarf French F^1 Hybrids. 6–8 in. (15–20 cm). There are several good ones among these such as Yellow Nugget and Seven Star Gold.

Mesembryanthemum criniflorum (Livingstone Daisy). 3–4 in. (9–10 cm). Thrives in the driest of places and loves full sun. Brilliant carmine, pink, salmon, and apricot shades. Pelleted seed.

Nemesia, Carnival. 9–12 in. (22–30 cm). Grows and flowers quickly, making a compact plant with large flowers in shades of bronze, crimson, scarlet, pink, orange, and yellow, besides white. Pelleted seed.

Nicotiana, Lime Green. 2 ft (60 cm). Outstanding variety of the Flowering Tobacco plant (not the sort for smoking). It is a good grower and useful for flower arrangements with its distinctive colour.

Pansy, International Prize Mixed. 6–9 in. (15–27 cm). Perennial but can be treated as HHA. Indeed, pansies make better flowers if grown afresh from seed each year. Seed sown outdoors in March or April will flower in summer. Prize Mixed includes pretty shades of blue, yellow, and bronze, besides near-white.

Petunia, F^1 multiflora, Colorama. 15–18 in. (37–45 cm). Compact plants suitable for border or window-box. Very free-flowering in blue, scarlet, salmon, pink, and white. There are also F^1 multiflora hybrids of many shades, such as Resisto Mixed with seed available as pellets.

Ricinus (Castor Oil Plant). 2–4 ft (60 cm–1·25 m). Most attractive foliage plant with leaves somewhat fig-leaf in shape but changing through green, bronze, and purple as they develop.

Rudbeckia (Gloriosa Daisy). 2–3 ft (60 cm–1 m). Some good double varieties make lovely subjects for use as cut flowers in late summer.

Ursinia, Anethoides Hybrids (HHA)

Arctotis, Harlequin (HHA)

Nicotiana, Lime Green (HHA)

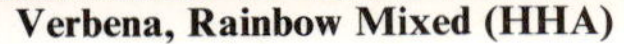
Verbena, Rainbow Mixed (HHA)

Ricinus, Mixed (HHA)

Stocks, Large-flowered Ten-week Mixed. 1 ft (30 m). Pelleted seed. From the wide and excellent choice of types in this long-popular and delightfully scented subject I make the choice because the pelleted seed makes it the easiest to raise.

Ursinia Anethoides. 12–15 in. (30–37 cm). Lovely double daisies in sparkling shades of chestnut-red and orange. These are ideal for a sun-baked spot.

Verbena, Rainbow Mixture. 9–12 in. (22–30 cm). Multi-flowered heads of dainty blooms bearing apricot, pink, lavender, crimson, scarlet, and other shades of colour. Useful in beds, border-edges, and window-boxes.

Zinnia, Peter Pan F^1 Hybrids. 1 ft (30 cm). Shades of pink, yellow, orange, cream, salmon-pink, and scarlet. Dwarfer still is Thumbelina, bright shades of double flowers, 4–6 in. (10–15 cm).

Petunia, Resisto Mixed (HHA)

Aster, Ostrich Plume Mixed (HHA)

10 The Pool

The nearest thing to a self-supporting garden is the garden pool, providing it is well sited, properly constructed, and stocked with the right balance of plants and fish. The plants take in carbon dioxide and breathe out oxygen, while the fish take in oxygen and breathe out carbon dioxide. This is only half the story and an over-simplification, but it indicates the possibility of creating a balance which will continue to maintain itself. Nor is the making of the pool the tough job it used to be when floor and walls had to be made of concrete, which needed to be made water-proof.

The modern method is to dig a hole, place a large waterproof sheet over it, run a hose into it, and watch the sheet steadily mould itself into whatever shape of hole you have constructed. And there is your pool. No precision is needed, because the weight of the water is enough to secure the sheet firmly so that it becomes a tightly clinging lining. The part of the sheet which remains overlapping the edge is hidden by paving stones or whatever similar materials you place on the narrow strip surrounding the pool. Once the pool is filled, and the water has had time to breathe out some of the stuff the local authority puts in to 'purify' it, you can put in your plants, housed in specially designed containers. When the plants have had time to firm themselves, so that the fish will not too readily pull them out, you can add your fish and call the job more or less complete.

Most garden pools seem to me rather small. The bigger the pool, the bigger the attraction and the more efficiently it will operate. The smaller the volume of water, the quicker it can heat up or cool down, hence the larger variation in temperature. Depth of pool must bear some relation to its surface area and I calculate that a pool should be approximately 18 inches deep up to an area of 50 square feet, and 2 feet deep up to 100 square feet (45 cm deep for 4·5 sq. m and 60 cm for 9 sq. m). Shape of pool is a matter of personal choice but in the small garden where the straight lines of the boundary fences and the house wall cannot be many yards from the pool, I think the pool edges should be curved. This may cause you to waste a little of the pool lining material, but not much – unless you go for extremely exaggerated curves.

Choose your site where it will get a reasonable amount of light but some respite from the heat of the noonday sun. That calls for a little shade on the south side, whether it be the garden fence or special plantings. My pool is sheltered by an arc of cypress trees. One reason for cypress is that it is evergreen, and it does not shower down loads of leaves on to the pool in autumn. Autumn leaves can be a menace, because their rotting in the water does no good. So let me emphasize that you should not put your pool beside a deciduous tree.

The area adjoining my pool provides a splash of colour at every season of the year, even in the depth of winter. The background of cypress not only improves the effect of the colour but also provide a shelter belt. And if you wonder why the water garden should be chosen as the site for all-year-round beauty of colour, the answer simply is that it is on the way to the greenhouse, which has to be visited every day of the year to check its occupants and record the temperatures inside and out. It is a pleasure to pause and watch the fish on one's way to and from the greenhouse.

Make the hole so that it will have a shelf or rim round the inside edge to take plants which want only shallow water – say 9 inches to 1 foot (22–30 cm) deep. There are several good plastics suitable for pool-liners. The cheapest is probably polythene but its disadvantage is that it does not weather so well as some of the more expensive ones. Your wisest course is to get a catalogue from a good firm of water-garden specialists. Such a catalogue will give you guidance on choice of liner, with hints on how to fix it, besides advice on the selection of plants and fish. Before buying your liner you must measure carefully all the area to be covered; the area of the pool bottom plus the side, plus the shelf, plus enough to sit on the surrounding surface to ensure a firm anchorage. Give all your measurements to the suppliers and they will make up a liner of the proper size.

Anchor the edges of the liner firmly all round, before starting to fill the pool, otherwise the in-flowing water may drag it in at one side instead of taking it down evenly. When you start the filling, use a hosepipe and let the water flow only slowly till you have the bottom well covered. Have as many helpers as necessary. The job is easiest with four of you, one to hold each of the four sides of the liner. Once the liner is sitting correctly on the floor of the pool you can turn on the tap to full pressure to fill up. My method is to fill up to within 3 inches (7 cm) of the brim at first. When all the plants and their containers have gone in, the water-level will rise. I like to leave a finished level of 1 to 2 inches below the rim – to allow for the sort of filling up which comes in a spell of rain.

How you cover the edge of the lining which lies on the ground round the pool depends on your taste. You need a firm surface on which you can stand at the pool edge, and this surfacing is the obvious thing to hide the liner edges and improve the tidiness of the pool's appearance. There are attractive, coloured

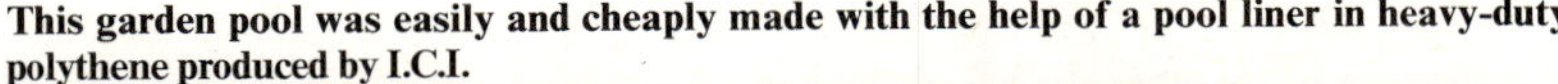

This garden pool was easily and cheaply made with the help of a pool liner in heavy-duty polythene produced by I.C.I.

paving slabs available, or you can buy second-hand paving stones from local authorities, or you can even make slabs of your own. The slabs are best laid so that they sink flush with the surrounding ground. This is especially so if the area is grassed down, as it allows the mower to go smoothly over the edge without trouble or risk of damage. It is advisable that the inside edge of the paving slabs should project over the pool edge by 2 or 3 inches (5–7 cm). To do this securely involves setting the slabs quite firmly, which is why I advise setting them on concrete rather than merely on soil or sand.

You can get some pretty looking and well-made pool linings which are prefabricated of rigid plastic or glass fibre. Their advantage is that they provide an elegant shape which is not easy to make by your own digging efforts. This may appeal to you, but I have to confess that I have *never* been able to make a success

Pools should have a little shade on the south side.

of installing any type of prefabricated pool, because I never get the hole the exact shape of the liner.

When you have filled your pool, given the water time to air, and begun to think of planting, you will realize why a shelf is needed round the inside edge of the pool. Some plants like fairly shallow water (we call them 'marginal plants') and we place these on the shelf. Even a deeper-going subject, such as the water-lily, does not always want its full depth at first. Stand its container on something to bring it temporarily near the surface (a brick will do) so that the leaves can float comfortably on the water. As the water-lily plant grows, it will want its full depth, which it can be given by removing the brick and letting the container settle on the floor.

Precise choice of plants is not a thing I advise inexperienced people to make for themselves. Although it is essential to take a proper interest, and to have a fair idea of what to plant, you can avoid mistakes by getting a plant collection made up by specialist water-garden nurserymen.

Water plants fall into several categories. There are the decorative, such as water irises; the shade-providers, such as floating plants, and the submerged oxygenators which help to keep the water right. Water-lilies, which go on the pool bottom, are both decorative and shade-giving. There are many attractive varieties and I suggest you consider Conqueror (rose-crimson), Candida (white and yellow centres), and Pygmaea helvola (a vigorous dwarf type with yellow flowers and mottled leaves). Another plant for the pool bottom (assuming the depth is not more than about 18 inches or 45 cm) is Aponogeton distachyum (Water Hawthorn) which has strongly scented white flowers.

For marginal plants you should include Calla palustris (Bog Arum) which has shiny, heart-shaped leaves, and flowers like small arum lilies; Iris laevigata (Water Iris) with sword-like leaves and flowers of clear violet-blue; and Myosotis palustris (Water Forget-me-not) whose dainty blue flowers come in pretty clusters. Two

As the pool is a focal point of your garden, aim at all-the-year-round colour in the area surrounding it.

good floating plants are Azolla caroliniana (Fairy Moss) which looks like a bronzy-green floating fern; and Lemna gibba, which is a thick duckweed with green and maroon fronds. Submerged oxygenators are absolutely essential and I suggest Elodea crispa (the curled anacharis) and Myriophyllum verticillatum which is a milfoil.

The best type of plant-container I have found for pools is an openwork plastic basket. This needs lining with something like hessian. Soil for water plants must not be rich because the nutrients in it would soon dissolve and cease to be available to the plants. They would also upset the chemical balance of the water and be bad for the fish. Nor must the soil have a large content of fibre or humus, the sort of stuff which is liable to float to the surface. Better have a stiffish soil, and you may be able to achieve this by using a substantial proportion of the subsoil which was dug out from the deeper part when you made the hole for the pool. After planting, put a layer of heavy gravel over the surface soil of the plant-container. This gravel not only helps to hold down the soil – reducing the float-off – but also discourages probing of the soil by inquisitive fish. Get your plants and their containers in time to have your pool planted up about three weeks before you bring in the fish. The plants should be firmly rooted before the fish arrive.

Numbers of fish will depend on the size of the pool, and a simple rough guide is to allow 6 inches of body-length of fish to every square foot of surface of water (15 cm to every 10 sq. dm). Since you will surely be hoping that your fish will breed, make allowance for that in calculating the initial stock. The fish-farm will have the answers worked out, and you can choose either a cheap buy (with longer to wait for spectacular results) or a more expensive buy with mature fish right from the start.

Popular characters include goldfish, with which I think everyone is familiar; shubunkins, large, colourful creatures with lots of blue about them; golden orfe, which my wife calls carrots (not inappropriately); and tench, for scavenging on the bottom of the pool. Besides these, you need water-snails to do more pond-cleaning work. Breeding pairs of any of the fishes cost a bit extra because they cannot be sorted out till they are about 5 to 6 inches (12–15 cm) long. You could buy a collection of small fish and adopt a policy of 'wait and see'. Or you could compromise by buying at least one breeding pair in your favourite line, whether goldfish, shubunkins, or something else.

Late autumn is a good time to start pool-making, ready for the planting season in May, and that would allow introduction of fish into the pool in late May or early June.

More questions come to me about greening of the pool water than about any other aspect of maintaining a garden pool. The greenness is due to algae whose growth is encouraged by alkalinity in the water and by excess of light. You cannot do much about the alkalinity if you have to fill the pool with water from the tap. But it should cure itself gradually by the interplay of other factors including the growth of the plants and the actions of the fish. Excess of light is usually corrected by midsummer if you have sufficient mature plants to cover the surface or shade it. Generally too, correct siting, to see that the pool is shaded from full sun, is a little help, though not enough in summer-time when even in partial shade the light is fairly strong. Where there is too much surface area exposed to light, and while you are waiting for your water-lilies to make enough big leaves, you can float a few small pieces of thin wood or other material on the surface.

Feeding the fish is a matter on which you will find the advice you need if you read the instructions on a packet of fish food. Over-feeding must be avoided, but in summer a daily feed is all right providing it is not overdone. I usually leave the food (in a submerged bowl) for about ten minutes and then discard any that has not been taken. You will find that the fish soon get into a routine and come dashing up to be fed. The kind of bowl I use is one whose sides curve inwards – it is really a dog's feeding-bowl. I use a small tin (top and bottom neatly cut out) down which to lower the food into the bowl (otherwise it would float). The food is not given until it has been soaked in water to make it swell: you don't want it swelling after it has got into the fish's stomach.

Severe frost is dangerous, not because the fish cannot stand the cold but for other reasons. For one thing, water expands on freezing and the ice can exert pressure which may become damaging. But what is more important is that ice seals the pond surface so that the water stagnates. You can get simple little heaters, with floats attached, run by electricity to keep a tiny hole open in the ice.

11 On the Rocks

Rock gardening is comparatively new: that is to say, gardening is as old as history knows of, while rock gardening came in only during the past century. One of the things which inspired it, probably, was complete informality – its unregimented appearance, as distinct from the many neat lines and geometric patterns with which earlier gardening was associated.

The common misconception concerning rock gardening is that it is just a matter of building up a heap of stones and making plants grow in crevices between them. Nothing could be wider of the mark. Indeed one might almost say the rock garden is a heap of *soil* camouflaged with stone and created to accommodate low-growing, creeping, or cascading plants. But neither picture is true, though the 'heap of soil' idea is nearer the mark. In rock gardening, stones are used to hide as much as possible of the soil surface, but the soil has to be there in ample quantity if the roots of the plants are to thrive.

Let us start with choice and nature of site, which should be the starting-point in any garden project. The rockery wants more than one face so that plants can look to different compass-points. In a small garden, this may not be easy. For instance you might want to cover a sloping face (between two garden levels) and that face obviously looks in only one direction. But you could at least build the rockery above the surface level of the higher ground so as to have a second face looking in the opposite direction. Another two points about choice of site are that you should have good drainage, which is where sloping ground is useful, and that you should have some degree of shade, at least for part of the day. It must be realized that stones absorb a great deal of heat, which makes for a heavy loss of moisture, and even though well-established roots should be clear of the hot surface, the leaves and stems can be affected, and there may be a great deal of water taken out by transpiration. Some shade against the noonday sun, therefore, is a worthwhile aim despite the fact that many rock plants like a fair share of sunshine.

Type of stone to use depends on what is available locally or at least not too far away. Stones are very heavy items and transport is not cheap. It is wise, therefore, in choosing the stone, to give high priority to transport costs. Apart from that, in whatever choice is available, you should aim at getting porous stones rather than any which are so hard and smooth that they are likely to shed water too readily.

One of the complaints sometimes made about rockeries is that they are difficult to weed. Let us look at that problem in two stages. First when the rockery is newly planted there are likely to be spots of soil exposed enough to catch and hold weed seeds which fall or blow on to it. When these seeds germinate the weeds are easy enough to recognize and can be pulled out with just a slight tug. The more tricky weed problem comes when the plants have established themselves and the weed pokes up in the middle of a clumpy plant. Such a weed may look very difficult to get out without seriously disturbing the rock plant. I suggest you first slip your fingers under the plant and you will probably find that its stems are merely

This charming rock-garden scene shows Aubrietia Spring Charm, the yellow Alyssum Mountain Gold and Iberis Sempervivens (white). In the background can be seen blue Myosotis, Purple Honesty, and the yellow, daisy-like flowers of Doronicum.

draping themselves over the ground and can be lifted a few inches so as to expose the weed's roothold. You can then get hold of it, and it will usually pull away without much effort. This is because the rambling rock plant, with its tendency to smother, does not allow the rival to get well established unless left too long. The next and more stubborn problem is to dispose of the weed which does get well established and cannot be uprooted without disturbing the roots of the rock plants. My answer is to apply either the herbicide, Weedol, or a hormone-type weedkiller of the kind used for killing lawn weeds. Obviously you cannot spray or water it on without killing your plants, but you can dab on the weedkiller with the help of a child's painting-brush.

One tip I would give here. Often we are told that the easy way is just to dab on the weedkiller straight from the bottle. I have done it myself, before experience taught me the error of it. An over-strong solution, and especially the concentrated chemical straight from the bottle, has a caustic effect which causes the leaves to collapse immediately. These collapsed leaves are unable to absorb the chemical to carry it down to the roots. So the strong dose will knock out the leaves but the roots will survive to send up new and perhaps even tougher growth. I advise you, therefore, to make up a proper solution, of the strength suggested for lawn-weeding, in some disposable container such as a small tin or plastic bottle. I emphasize the need for using a disposable container, because it is dangerous to keep any mixture or solution that is left over. It might later be mistaken for almost anything.

Throw it into the dustbin, container and all, when you have finished dabbing the tricky weeds.

Someone is sure to say that the whole idea of spot treatment of rockery weeds is impractical because the weeds are often in physical contact with the plants and spot treatment of the weeds will involve getting some of the weedkiller on the plants. The answer is to improvise so that you can isolate the plants from the treatment given to the weeds. One way is to use a plastic carton, such as a cream carton, stuff some cotton wool into the bottom, and soak the cotton wool with the lawn weedkiller. If that carton is placed upside-down, over the weed, the weed-killer will do its work without any risk to adjoining plants. It is also possible to cover plants with polythene for protection while applying herbicides to weeds near by.

As in any other part of the garden, you are bound to have a few pests. Rockeries naturally attract slugs, because such creatures love the moist shade they can enjoy by sitting on the stones under the mat of plant growth. Modern slug baits can be put where the slugs can get at them but where neither birds nor domestic pets will be at risk. A piece of tile, propped up no higher than ½ inch (13 mm) at one end, can be tucked under plant growth and slug pellets can be put under the tile. Or you can pour liquid slug-killer on the soil round the plant roots. One little trick which helps control both weeds and slugs is to get some small sharp gritty gravel and give a lavish covering of this to the soil round each plant as you do the planting.

Another common pest in some rockeries is the ant. Ants live in colonies and work extremely hard. Apart from the upset they cause by their tunnelling and the discomfort they can give when the bite, they nurse greenfly, to ensure that your garden never goes short of them. So it is wise to use some ant-killer whenever you see ants moving about near your rockery. A safe answer is one of the modern baits such as Nippon (a sticky liquid) or Tugon (fine granules). Instructions with both tell you how to ensure that you do not put children or pets at risk when you use these pesticides.

Choice of plants for the rockery is almost endless, especially if it is a large rockery, because plenty of subjects normally grown in various parts of the garden can be accommodated if large enough pockets of soil are available to take their roots. People generally refer to rock plants as 'alpines' but this rather loose description is not accurate. Some of our best rockery plants come from warmer areas than the Alps and some true alpines could not stand our winters! (Don't forget plants can find life snug under snow sometimes.) One rock plant of which I am very fond is Androsace, and this one strongly dislikes wet winters. It is worth protecting in winter with a sheet of glass or rigid plastic propped up to throw off the rain. To be more elaborate, you could cover with a cloche. But never close up the cloche completely, as ample ventilation is necessary. On the other hand, I don't like to see a cloche set into place with both ends wide open. This makes a kind of wind tunnel and the draught can be damaging.

Here is a useful selection:

Alyssum saxatile, a perennial with golden-yellow flowers, sometimes known as Gold Dust. There is a variety, Citrinum, whose flowers are more lemon-coloured.

Androsace sarmentosa is the Rock Jasmine. It sends out runners which make lovely hummocks smothered in rose-pink flowers.

Arabis albida, the Rock Cress is a white-flowered trailer which grows vigorously and flowers freely without any attention.

Armeria, sometimes known as Thrift and sometimes as the Sea Pink, likes seaside conditions. Its foliage is grass-like and makes a good contrast amid broader-leaved subjects.

Aubrieta is too well known to need much description. It trails and rambles freely and keeps up a lovely show of colour, usually a purple-lavender shade. But there are several varieties available, with pink and red ones included.

Ceratostigma plumbaginoides is the Leadwort, blue of course, and is one of the easiest of all rock plants, and has won the Royal Horticultural Society's Award of Garden Merit.

Dianthus. Many people know dianthus as a garden pink and perhaps Dianthus barbatus (Sweet William) but I do not think the Rock Pink is as well known as it deserves to be. Varieties like Allwoodii alpinus (mixed) 9–12 inches (22–30 cm), and Brilliancy (crimson-scarlet) 6 inches (15 cm), are delightful rock plants.

Doronicum, the Leopard's Bane, is another well-known subject. For the rockery you should go for Doronicum cordatum which grows only 6 inches (15 cm) tall, has bright yellow flowers, and enjoys the shadier side.

Helianthemum, the Rock Rose, comes in several good varieties and one I like very much is Fireball which has double flowers in crimson.

Iberis, the perennial candytuft should be dotted about in places where its bold mass of white bloom will highlight brighter colours round it.

Lithospermum, also known as Gromwell, a trailer which gives a good display all summer and I particularly recommend the variety Grace Ward for its rich blue, large flowers.

Polygonum vaccinifolium has bright pink flowers on stems which trail delightfully.

Finally, please note that several of the bulbous subjects described in Chapter 7, and the dwarf annuals mentioned in Chapter 9 are well suited for growing in the rockery.

12 Fruit

TREE FRUITS

In garden conditions, most fruit is so easy to grow that one might almost say it looks after itself. By 'garden conditions' I mean that the skill and labour needed to maintain commercial crops is neither necessary nor profitable in the garden. I am not advocating neglect, but I am aware that the effect of ensuring a 100 per cent perfect crop of, say, apples in the home garden will cost a great deal of money on spraying materials and a great deal of time. And in the end one mature standard or large bush will produce a crop bigger than can be eaten by the family and friends before it goes bad.

The message is that if the gardener adopts a reasonable standard of cleanliness and tidiness in his garden he will be able to harvest a crop which will more than meet his needs. He will have a few to discard as not worth eating; a few which, though imperfect, will keep long enough for him to use them; and the remainder good enough to put into store. That remainder should maintain a supply for as long as one could expect fruit to keep in store. I explain this because people are constantly asking me how to keep their fruit trees absolutely clear of pests and diseases. Such an aim is almost hopeless, apart from being uneconomic. The correct approach, as in almost all gardening, is to keep pests and disease under control rather than attempt to eliminate them. It is in that spirit that we must approach the problem of deciding what role fruit can play in the busy man's garden. And since the apple is perhaps the most popular of our garden fruits, let us look at that first.

Originally, apples were grown on their own roots or on crab-apple rootstocks: that is to say, some were grafted on to young trees of crab-apples. As the chosen variety grew, the shoot of crab-apple above the point of graft was cut clean off. Thus, although the root system and the base of the trunk were of crab-apple, the upper part, which produced the fruiting branches, was of the variety of the grower's choosing. This grafting was done because the crab-apple was known to be able to produce a vigorous root system which would be the foundation of a good tree. There were two disadvantages in the use of crab stock. One was that it made a big tree (too big for today's suburban garden) and the other was that it was a long time coming to fruition. Trees are not expected to give full crops of fruit till they reach their mature size, and a big tree obviously takes longer than a little one to grow up.

Later, came the discovery that apples could be grafted successfully on to much dwarfer-growing subjects. These cancelled out both disadvantages of the crab. That is, they needed less space and they were quicker to reach fruition. The possibilities of the uses of these dwarfing stocks were soon exploited and we found that we could grow apples in the garden on trees shaped as low hedges. Some shapes were called cordons, some espalier, and some by other descriptive names. Parallel discoveries were being made with pears so that they too were soon being grown as tidy little trees suitable for the smallest garden.

All this is still true, and you will find many dwarf espaliers and cordons producing apples and pears in gardens today. You will also find some that are badly misshapen (out of control, in fact) and many that produce little or no fruit. The fault does not lie with the researchers and nurserymen who discovered and produced these dwarf specimens. The trouble is that pruning to keep them shapely and fruitful demands a great deal of skill – and time to practise it. In these hectic days, people have much more exciting things to do in their leisure time and they have neither the skill for this type of fruit-growing, nor the will to acquire it.

The technique of dwarfing has lost none of its popularity, but the other dwarf shapes now attract more attention, especially the half-standard and the bush. Don't confuse 'bush' with a little thing like a rose bush; it is a definition of shape rather than of size. The original shape, often seen in woodland trees, is called 'standard' which means a tree whose branches start about head height (5–6 ft or 1·5–2 m) so that one can walk under the tree without hitting one's head on the branches. Fruit-picking from such trees is all ladder-work.

Pear, Conference

The half-standard is a similar shape to the standard except that its branches start lower down ($3\frac{1}{2}$–4 ft or 1–1·25 m from the ground) so that one cannot walk under them. The 'bush' tree is one with about $2\frac{1}{2}$ ft (75 cm) of trunk and with branches growing at an angle which make a sort of goblet-shape of tree. There are trees called 'dwarf bush', which means that their shape is the same as that I have described as 'bush' but that they are smaller. Their branches do not spread so widely nor so high. Today's 'standard' shape of fruit tree is not so big as the old types on crab stock, except perhaps with extremely vigorous varieties – Bramley for instance.

So what shape does the busy gardener choose? The dwarf bush is the easiest, in my reckoning, because it is small enough for easy maintenance and easy picking, and yet simple enough to call for no artful pruning. The emphasis is on 'dwarf', because I have some normal bush-shaped trees

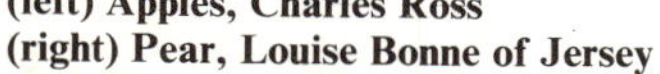

(left) Apples, Charles Ross
(right) Pear, Louise Bonne of Jersey

Cherries, Early Rivers

which have a diagonal spread of 20 ft (6 m) and which need ladders to reach their top branches. I do not rule out a modern 'standard' shape of tree providing the garden is not too small for it. Modern standards are worked on rather less vigorous stocks than the old crab, so providing you don't go for too vigorous a variety you get a manageable tree. There are several reasons why I do not rule it out. The standard makes a pleasant feature and its spread does no harm because one can walk under it and the area it occupies at ground-level is quite insignificant. It does not interfere with grass-mowing, and it offers a useful bit of shade when one wants to sit outdoors in a deckchair on a sunny day. Its only disadvantage is that it needs a ladder at times.

Most of what I have said about apples and their tree shapes applies also to pears, but I am not keen on asking the busy gardener to grow pears. They are not as simple as apples when it comes to picking the fruit and getting it exactly right for eating. A pear picked too early will not ripen properly, and if it is left till just the right time for picking it will probably be damaged by bird-pecking, so that instead of ripening up to readiness for eating it goes off. Pears must be finished off carefully after picking, whereas apples rarely need more than a normal garage or shed as a storage place to see them through to readiness for good eating.

For those of you who may be puzzled, let me explain that there are three ripeness stages with apples and pears: ripe for picking, ripe for eating, and seed-ripe (which means rotten). A few apple varieties are ready to eat when picking-ripe, others require varying lengths of time to finish off after picking. The test of 'picking-ripeness' is easy enough. You take a gentle hold of the fruit in the palm of your hand (no gripping with the fingers) and lift it up through an angle of ninety degrees (that is, from the perpendicular or hanging position to the horizontal). But while you lift you should be twisting it to the same extent, through ninety degrees. It is a single, lift-and-twist movement, and not two separate movements. If the fruit is ready to leave the tree, it will come away when you give it that movement. If not, the one specimen you have tested may have become loosened so that it will end by falling off a couple of days later; so don't go around the tree testing every fruit.

Before you can hope to do any picking, you must choose and plant your tree – or perhaps I ought to say 'trees' in the plural. Although some varieties of apple and pear are classed as self-fertile, it is generally true that they crop better when cross-pollinated; that is to say when, with the help of bees and other insects, the pollen from the blossom of one variety is carried to the blossom of another. In suburban gardens this problem is not as critical as is sometimes believed, providing there are fruit trees in neighbouring gardens. The bees do not recognize garden boundaries and they work busily through a group of gardens, transferring pollen in a neighbourly fashion so that the fruit in one garden helps the fruit in another.

One pollination solution is simple, and that is to plant a multi-variety tree. Such a tree is one on which three to five different varieties have been grafted so that they give the grower a choice of fruit and at the same time solve the cross-pollination problem. But for the easy-going, or the man in a hurry, the multi-tree (sometimes called a 'Family Tree') can be a problem. Since varieties differ in vigour, and some factors can accentuate those differences, a tree may become unbalanced, and the weaker varieties can die out. Correcting the balance is not a matter of simple pruning. Hard pruning encourages vigorous new growth and the strong variety will come up stronger instead of slowing down when you try to keep it in check by cutting it back. There are ways of doing it, if you know when and how to prune, but I just can't class that as easy gardening. Single-variety trees are much easier to manage.

It is wise to take the advice of your nurseryman on choice of variety and also on choice of rootstock, because a rootstock which is ideal for one variety may not be the best choice for another variety. If a Cox on 111 rootstock were planted at the same time as a Tydeman's Early on 106 rootstock they would develop in tree size as like as two peas. This would be due to the fact that the more vigorous variety (Tydeman's) was on the more dwarfing stock (106).

Tell your nurseryman all you can about the position of your garden (high or low, sheltered or exposed) and its type of soil. Make up your mind whether you want to grow any of the varieties you normally see in the shops or whether you would rather have something different. I think you will want to avoid late, long-keeping varieties because they need storing and watching. I don't think there is much point in growing what we call 'cookers'. (Any apple will cook, but some are not good for eating raw.) My tip would be to consider Laxton's Fortune for September/October eating and Egremont Russet for October/November eating. I find both these pretty trouble-free. For pears, I should go for Williams (September) and Conference (November), but beware of the problems I have mentioned. You may have difficulty in getting the so-called 'standard' shape of tree because there is not much demand for them. Nurserymen cannot afford to use ground for growing stuff which is not going to sell well. When you buy dwarf bushes I suggest you ask for what are described as 'three-year' trees. These will have had the necessary pruning to give them the starting shape you want.

Most writers advocate shortening all the shoots at planting time, but frankly I advise leaving them alone. This advice is based on long experience and the reasoning is this. A newly planted tree has to make a good deal of root growth to get itself anchored and settled in. Root growth is directly related to the amount of shoot and leaf growth which is available to support it. So, with the sort of tree I am advising you to buy, you will get better and quicker root development if you plant it just as you get it, with no pruning of your own. You must make an exception where an odd shoot has been damaged at some stage before you complete the planting. Invariably, damaged wood should be snipped off. What I have said about planting trees without pruning is not a general rule for all trees of all sizes. But it certainly applies to young trees such as I have described which have had their initial shaping completed in the nursery.

Planting need not involve the amount of hard work which many people make of it. If you were trying to establish an orchard in a rough old field there would be much work needed to ensure the success of the venture. But in a garden where there has been reasonable cultivation going on, there is no need for elaborate preparation before planting a tree. You may be advised to do all sorts of deep digging and burying of barrow-loads of manure. It can't do the soil much harm and it may do you some good if you need exercise. But really, and again I emphasize that I am referring to reasonable garden soil, I have no time for such luxury. Nor is there any need for great excavation, as if you were planning to bury an old camel. The planting hole wants to be about a spade's depth, which is 9 to 10 inches (22–25 cm), and wide enough to allow for a reasonable spread of root. A 3-foot (1 m) diameter hole is usually ample and any root too long for that will suffer nothing from being neatly shortened with a sharp knife or pair of secateurs.

The soil at the bottom of the hole should be forked up to make sure it is not rock-hard. Some peat or leafmould forked into it will help to prevent its binding too hard and tight later. The tree needs setting in the hole with roots spread outwards (not downwards) and the soil wants to be put back carefully round the roots. With the tree held by its main stem (or trunk) it should be shaken up and down gently to get soil under the roots to support it in a position which leaves it no deeper than it was in its former home. There will be a soil-mark to show you its old planting level. I do not fuss about fertilizer at planting time, but simply sprinkle a normal dressing of a high-potash fertilizer (about 4 ounces to the square yard – 25 grams to the square metre) on the surface and let the rain wash it down. The tree's feeding roots work in the surface soil (the top 9 inches (22 cm)) and not in the depths.

Be sure you know the planting distance. Your nurseryman will tell you. Not that you will be planting your trees in rows, but because you need to allow sufficient distance for your tree to develop without getting into the way of other things and without being too close to a hedge or a path. With all tree-planting, as with buying small puppies, it is easy to be deceived into thinking that you are allowing too much space. Space which looks as if it is being wasted can be filled with something dispensable which can be removed later.

At the beginning of the chapter I mentioned the folly of trying to achieve total elimination of pests and disease. Fuller details of equipment and sprays needed for these matters are dealt with later in the book, but for your peace of mind, if you think of planting fruit trees, I assure you now that little spraying is needed in average garden conditions. An aphicide is useful at bud burst, which is when the first bits of green start showing on the stems in spring, and perhaps another pesticide is helpful when the blossom petals have fallen. Apart from that, I suggest you need neither go looking for trouble with a magnifying glass nor sloshing loads of chemicals on to your trees. It does not need a very sharp eye to detect real trouble when it begins to show up: and pest control these days does not involve knowing all sorts of complicated chemicals. Some sprays are called simply 'General Garden Fungicide' and 'Pest Spray for Fruit and Vegetables'. So when you plant a tree, don't get worried into thinking you are planting trouble or that you are going to have to take a course of study on chemicals and their uses.

Plums are easy trees to grow, though you have to accept that they can have their off-years and that sometimes in a glut year they suffer from branch breakage due to weight of crop. The variety Victoria is still my favourite both for ease of growing and for enjoyment. It eats well straight off the tree; it is easy to put down in the deep freeze if you have one.

Peach is another easy subject, except that like the plum it can have its off-years. The chief trouble with the peach is that it blooms too early to escape the frosts. I grow one on a northerly aspect so that it does not catch the morning sun. This avoids having frosted blossom thawed out too rapidly and thereby being ruined. Peaches grow so well from stones that if you can wait about five years for the fruit you might get a pleasant surprise. I do not advise growing peach trees too dwarf, because spring frost strikes worst near the ground. If the tree's head is well up in the air, but shaded from early sun, the chance of fruiting is improved.

Although I grow figs and quinces successfully, I will not advise these for easy gardening. Not that they are difficult subjects, but they need certain attention at the right time which is hard on the casual gardener.

There is nothing difficult about the growing of cherries, but birds just won't let them ripen. I get no cherries from my trees, except for the few saved by my wife's trick of slipping an old nylon stocking over a branch. I really think it is too much trouble to save cherries from the birds so I say the busy gardener may as well forget them.

Raspberries, Lloyd George

Plums, Belle de Louvain

Plums, Warwickshire Drooper

BUSH FRUITS

Apart from the tree fruits, there are other fruits suitable for the small garden, and several of them demand little enough attention to make them worth putting on the casual gardener's list. Three that I would recommend are raspberries, black currants, and gooseberries. All ought to be fed – like the rest of the garden – and one cannot guarantee that they will differ from other subjects in proneness to the occasional pest or disease attack. But the attention they need is little and simple.

Consider first the raspberry. You plant it, cut it down to near ground-level, and wait. Next year it will make strong stems (canes) but no fruit. You will be expected to shorten stems which have grown too tall or are bent over in bad shape. Most enthusiasts advise that you stake them, but in any reasonably sheltered garden, a row of healthy raspberry canes should stand up fairly well for themselves. In the following season when you have gathered the fruit, you cut out (down to ground-level) those canes which have given fruit. Ah, you will ask, but how does one know which are the fruited canes? It sounds a problem, because there will be as many new stems (canes) growing in your raspberry row as there will be older canes

Red currants, Laxton's No. 1

which have finished fruiting. But in practice it is no problem at all, because the canes which have done the fruiting will have dull, scruffy leaves, while the new shoots will have bright green fresh-looking leaves. It boils down to a simple annual routine of cutting out the canes from which you have gathered fruit, and lightly trimming any new ones whose tips are bending in directions where they are not wanted.

Raspberries should be planted about 18 inches (45 cm) apart, in a row running from north to south, if possible. This is to allow the sun to reach both sides of the row – the east side during the first half of the day and the west side later. If a row of such tall plants runs from east to west, the northern side is robbed of sun. However, in a small garden the rule does not have to be obeyed if it is inconvenient, providing only a single row is grown. East–west planting would mean that the fruit would almost all grow on the sunny side but this would not seriously reduce the size of crop. If you must plant more than one row, and the rows have to run in the wrong direction, I suggest you keep the rows far enough apart, so that one does not shade the other. Sucker shoots from raspberries will pop up all along the rows and sometimes several feet from their mother plants. These suckers can be dug up in autumn and planted to provide a fresh row. Any not wanted for this purpose should be chopped down as soon as they appear.

Apart from the consideration of how to orientate the row, I suggest that a row of raspberries will make an excellent dividing screen. It can be used to separate one part of the vegetable garden from another, or to separate decorative garden from vegetable garden. My favourite variety remains Lloyd George, with Malling Jewel as second choice, and September for early autumn picking.

Black currants have one thing in common with raspberries in that the only pruning needed is when they finish their season's fruiting. Indeed, my wife and I have an easy drill for pruning and fruit-picking as a joint effort in one operation. I snip off the shoots which are loaded with fruit and pass them to her to strip the currants off the stems. When we finish, the bushes are pruned, the crop is picked, and the old stems are on the bonfire. So the whole job is cleared up with virtually nothing more to do for another year. The basis of the harvest-time pruning is similar to that for the raspberry except that the growth habit of the two subjects is not quite the same. Whereas replacement canes of raspberry (to carry the following year's crop) spring from ground-level, the new shoots of black currant spring from anywhere along the mature (and fruiting) stem. So with currants one must not cut out the fruiting stem completely, but merely cut it down by about two-thirds, to a suitable, outward-pointing new shoot. There will be a few sprigs of currants to gather from points below the pruning-mark. But you can see how simple it all is. Boskoop Giant and Wellington XXX are my choice of varieties. If you use black currants as a hedge, they should be planted 4–5 feet (1·25–1·5 m) apart and if you put them alongside a path, plant them 2½ feet (75 cm) from the edge of the pathway.

Red currants, by the way, have a different habit of growth from that of black currants. Their wood is more permanent, more like that of an apple tree, so they must be pruned carefully and not just cut clean out after fruiting. I rule them out of the easy-gardening list. However, as a point of interest rather than a piece of sound advice, I experimented by leaving a short row of red currants entirely unpruned for seven years. Cropping continued to be fairly good. After that period, the bushes were trimmed.

Some people reckon that loganberries, blackberries, and similar fruits are easy subjects. They are certainly easy in the sense that they will fruit well without skilled attention. But they are time-consumers because they make long growths which have to be disciplined, by training in the desired direction and tying them securely to keep them in place. This is an extra nuisance with the thorny characters, but it is bad enough with my thornless varieties of loganberry and blackberry. So I am not including these and several other pleasant hybrid berries in the list for the casual gardener.

I am in a quandary about strawberries. They are so highly appreciated that one hates to leave them out, but to class them as a good choice for the busy man's garden would not be right. I will compromise by telling you the easiest (but not the cheapest) way I know of growing them; and leave you to make your own decision. Buy young plants from a good nursery in August/September. My favourite variety after all these years is still Royal Sovereign. Plant them 1 foot (30 cm) apart and allow 3 feet (1 m) between rows. Cover with cloches in February, to keep them clear of rain splashes and to make them crop early.

Gooseberry bushes are prickly things, but in the right part of the garden, where they will not snag people's stockings, their prickly nature is insignificant. When you pick the fruit you can lift a branch gently by its tip, and take the fruit from under the branch without getting yourself scratched at all. Choose a spot where the bushes can be used as dividers; that is, as a hedge to separate one bit of garden from another. But avoid a place where you need to move frequently along either side of the division. Once planted and reasonably fed, I find them no trouble. Pruning calls for no skill. Common sense tells you when to remove shoots that are causing overcrowding. The skilled grower varies his pruning according to the habit of the variety; opening the middle of the bush if it is an upright grower and shortening the low branches if the variety is inclined to make a spreading, droopy bush. But experience has taught me that lack of such refinement need not rob anyone of good pickings. Therefore, I class the gooseberry as a suitable subject for the labour-saver's garden.

Give the bushes plenty of space. A 5-foot (1·5 m) diameter circle is wanted for each, and I should not centre the plant nearer than 3 feet (1 m) from any pathway where people have to walk frequently. A plant so centred will come near enough to the path edge as it matures. Golden Drop is my favourite dessert variety. After that, I choose Leveller (yellow-green) and Whinham's Industry (red).

13 Vegetables

Fashions change rather less in gardening than in many subjects but they do change. There was a time when the garden was looked upon as an essential source of food for the family. Then flowers began to get a bigger share of the space, and lawns too. Each major war has seen a rush back to maximum food production, and peace has usually brought a reaction back towards more beauty – flowers and lawn.

When prepacked vegetables came in, they at first displaced the home-grown. As people began to tire of the sameness of prepacked foods, the desire for the flavour and freshness of home-grown food revived. Next came world inflation, with rising prices for many foods, and this gave more impetus to the rising demand for 'home-grown' to help the family budget.

Whichever of these points appeals most to you – and I write only as a gardener and not as an economist – there is absolutely no doubt that the trend in home growing of vegetables is definitely upwards.

Yet we still have a fair amount of affluence. Much time is occupied in commuting. There are exciting distractions. Husband and wife may both go out to work. Week-ends are devoted to

(above left) Broad Bean, Dreadnought
(below left) Runner Bean, As Long as Your Arm
(below) Aubergine (Egg Plant), Long Purple

so-called 'relaxation' (the mad rush round which creates more tension than comfort). Where amid all this do we fit in the gardening? What we are sure of is that people do love gardening. They want to spend less time (though perhaps more money) on it. With all these points in mind we must aim at growing as many vegetables as we can, and for the busy or casual gardener we must first look for those which are easier, but we must also consider the importance of those which quickly lose flavour if not eaten straight from the garden. Value for money, in terms of yield per square yard of ground, is another consideration. Nor must we forget that some things are heavy to hump, so even a potato may have its place in the garden for the labour it saves in carrying from the shops.

Sometimes there is confusion as to what is a fruit and what is a vegetable. Having mentioned the tomato as a vegetable, let me say that botanically the part of it we eat is the fruit, but horticulturally it is classed as a vegetable, and so for our purpose a vegetable it is. A vegetable is a plant from which we may eat the root (carrot), the stem (rhubarb), the leaves (lettuce), the seeds (peas), or the flowers (cauliflower). A fruit plant is one from which we normally eat only the fruit.

Undue weight is sometimes given these days to controversial arguments about lack of flavour in vegetables. Plant-breeders have to consider many factors, and some of them, such as uniformity of size and evenness of ripening, have nothing to do with flavour. But flavour is high on the list of factors which the breeder aims at all the time, no matter what other qualities he is trying to change. Some complaints about lack of flavour have no standing at all, because they come from chain-smokers and other people who do not give their palates a chance. But many genuine complaints come from people who do not realize when or where to expect flavour

(top) Broccoli, St George
(above) Brussels Sprouts, Prince Askold
(below) Cabbage, Ornamental

to be at its best. So far as most vegetables are concerned, feeding, timing, and other skilled attention by the market-gardener usually ensure flavour, but the flavour can be lost on its way to you through the shops. I have found delicious flavour in vegetables from a local market-garden, even among varieties sometimes condemned as having no flavour. Freshness was the secret.

Flavours vary and being human we have our prejudices. But we must not let those prejudices cause us to refuse to try new varieties of vegetables. And to give them a fair test, we must pick and eat them fresh. Testing a selection of varieties, instead of sticking grimly to an old favourite, helps to discover those which suit our soil and conditions. If you grow these reasonably well, and eat them fresh, they will have a better flavour than those you carry home from the market.

Almost all vegetables are easy to grow, but that would not justify packing the whole range into a garden designed for anyone who wants his gardening to be leisurely. The answer is to be highly selective, and to grow just those few which appeal most and which you feel you can make time to look after. How you make your selection depends on whether you put the emphasis on time-saving, or providing freshness, or on some sort of compromise. With that in mind, the aim here should not be to run through the whole catalogue but rather to suggest a comprehensive list, with sufficient guidance on each item to allow you to make a happy choice.

Items defined as easy may occupy a great deal of time when grown by an enthusiast. You should see the work people put into growing a prize-winning parsnip or some long, straight runner beans. But it is fair to class a subject as easy if it *can* be grown without hard work or long hours of attention. On that basis, consider the following and make a choice (small or large) from the list:

Jerusalem artichoke, broad bean, french bean, runner bean, sprouting broccoli, brussels sprout, cabbage, carrot, courgette, outdoor cucumber, lettuce, onion, pea, potato, radish, rhubarb, shallot, tomato, vegetable marrow, and a small selection of herbs.

Jerusalem artichoke. A root vegetable like a badly shaped potato with a slightly smoky flavour. (The variety Fuseau is not smoky.) Makes a plant like a sunflower, which grows quickly and flowers. Useful to provide a quick screen to hide the compost-heap, even if you don't care much for the vegetable when harvested. Dig up in late autumn, or as required. Save a few to replant at planting time, which is February.

Broad bean. Sow the variety Aquadulce early in November in a double row 6 inches (15 cm) each way. They stand the winter and give good pickings in early summer. For spring sowing (February and March) include The Midget and Exhibition Longpod.

French dwarf bean. Sow the variety Tendergreen in late April, 6 inches (15 cm) apart in a single row. Pick the beans 4–6 inches (10–15 cm) long, when they are stringless and tender. Cook them whole.

Runner bean. Does best in milder districts. Hammond's Dwarf sown in mid-May will grow without staking. The beans will not be long, straight specimens like those grown on sticks. For growing on tall sticks, good varieties include As Long as Your Arm, Streamline, and Yardstick. Sow about 8 inches (20 cm) apart. Put two rows of sticks 1 foot (30 cm) apart and draw them together, with ties, at the top.

Purple sprouting broccoli. Sow in April in a straight row and thin out to 18 inches

(45 cm) apart as they grow. Watch out for caterpillars, aphis, and perhaps rootfly, but the remedy can fit into an easy pesticide routine. The purplish flower-heads are good for eating in spring. They don't stay as whole tight heads like cauliflowers, but break up into shoots which cook green and tender.

Brussels sprout. Likes a long season of growth and should be sown in March for planting early in May. Needs fairly rich but really firm ground. Loose ground encourages flabby sprouts instead of hard tight buttons. Never pick too many at a time from one plant if picking for the daily needs. Take the lowest sprouts from each plant all along the row. Varieties: Early Dwarf, Exhibition, and Peer Gynt.

Cabbage. You can go to a great deal of trouble over cabbage and make it pay you, as I do, by giving good pickings of greenstuff all the year round. Or you can take the easy course and just go for a couple of varieties. Sow a summer variety such as Velocity in February and get firm tender hearts in summer just when you feel the need for a change from the endless salads. Next, sow in late July or August a variety such as Springtide which will stand all winter to give you those lovely blood-cooling greens you need in spring.

Carrot. Here again, repeated sowings can ensure year-round supplies but if you don't want that trouble, at least sow a few Amsterdam Forcing under a row of cloches in early March. These carrots are excellent grated, uncooked, in summer salads.

Courgette: *see* Vegetable marrow.

Cucumber. At its best this is an indoor vegetable, but you can raise good specimens outdoors from an early June planting. Buy plants of a Ridge cucumber such as Greenline or a gourmet hybrid called Kyoto and plant 30 inches (75 cm) apart.

Lettuce. The choice of varieties is confusing, especially if you prefer to leave most lettuce production to the commercial grower who does the job so well. Nevertheless, it is good to have a few of your own in high summer, when the heat is liable to make the market stocks go a bit limp. Easy drill is to get a packet of mixed varieties. Make three or four sowings at fortnightly intervals. Just small sowings – about 2 yards (2 m) of row at a time. Sow first under the cloches with the carrots.

Onion: *see* Shallot.

Pea. This vegetable has come a long way since it was first introduced to this country as a so-called 'dainty dish for ladies'. The easy drill is to settle on one variety. Choose an early, and make it a dwarf so that it needs no staking. Little Marvel fills the bill. 'Early' does not mean that it is no use mid-season or late, but merely that it grows and matures quickly. Perhaps some slower varieties produce better crops, but go for the easy life. Start sowing Little Marvel in March in a flat-bottomed drill. Scatter the peas 2–3 inches (5–7 cm) apart in the drill and cover with 2 inches of soil.

Potato. I am not advocating that you grow all your own potatoes or even any substantial quantity. The only argument in favour of that would be that they are a heavy crop to carry long distances. That does not matter if you can buy where there is only a short haul. Being a keen gardener, and having ample space, I grow all my own.

What I enjoy most is that first small dishful dug up in summer to be eaten, suitably dressed with parsley butter, with a fresh green salad. Even the busiest of gardeners could find room for half a dozen seed potatoes (1 lb (0·5 kg) in total weight). They will go in a row a couple of yards long and you need not earth them up. The variety I find easy and prolific is Arran Pilot.

Cabbage, Spring, Wheelers Imperial

Cabbage, Stonehead

Radish. No one can say that radish needs any growing at all. Indeed all you need do is use radish seeds as markers along the rows in which you sow other seeds (flowers or vegetables). They come up quicker than most things, thereby marking the row and helping you remember what sowing you have done. If you want to sow them separately, it is quite easy to pop in a short row occasionally, but do keep the row short (2 yards (2 m)) because a radish wants to be eaten as soon as ready and not left to get big or coarse. A new variety called Cherry Belle is a quick grower, crisp and tasty.

Rhubarb. This is something you can find no excuse for leaving out. Victoria and Champagne are reliable. Plant the roots in early March, 3 feet (1 m) apart, and see that they are not on hungry soil. Never pull too many sticks at a time from

Cauliflower, Snowdrift

Radish, Cherry Belle

Celery, American Green

one plant or you will weaken it. See that you leave always much more growth than you remove.

Shallot. This is another of those vegetables which you more or less plant and forget. It starts off as a round bulb which you plant shallowly – more of it standing out of the ground than below surface level – and as it settles into growth it sits on the surface with only its roots in the soil. Growth begins as lots of green hollow shoots the bases of which swell so that by the end of the season's growth you have a cluster of bulbs sitting looking at you at every spot where you planted a single

Tomato, Craigella

bulb. It is such a useful vegetable that it would be worth growing even if it were difficult. When the green shoots have made what growth you want, say 6 inches (15 cm) or more, you can pull up a shallot whenever you fancy, for what we call 'spring onions' – those green onions used in salads. Shallots are milder than the onions normally raised for this purpose.

In our garden we make full use of shallots. Some we pull green as described. When the crop is ripe – indicated by the dying down of the green tops – we lift and sort into three categories according to size. The smallest we pickle, the medium size we save to plant for next year's crop, and the largest we cook. Like the green ones used as spring onions, the flavour in the picklers and the larger cookers is milder than that of the onion. And it is a good flavour.

I have listed shallots before **onions** because the drill I have explained for planting them applies to onions grown from what we call *sets*. These are small bulbs which make growing extremely easy. But I advise you not to plant onion sets till March. Put them about 5 inches (12 cm) apart in rows a foot (30 cm) apart. If you want to grow onions from seed you can start the seed earlier under glass or sow outdoors in March. Incidentally, if a seedhead appears in a shallot or an onion, nip it out straight away and you will still get a usable plant.

Tomato. I have already put the tomato high on the list for even the casual gardener. Raising them the easy way, as distinct from doing everything according to the book, may mean a smaller over-all crop and a few under-sized fruits, but the crop will still be worth while. Outdoors, choose a spot beside a sunny wall because the tomato loves warmth and comfort at all times, and the season of suitable outdoor weather is so short that any help to speedier growth is useful.

Prepare the ground so that you can set the row of plants a good 2 feet (60 cm) from the wall. I plant a little closer, but then the wall acts like blotting-paper so I have to give extra attention to watering. I reckon that at 2 feet (60 cm) clear, the plants can find enough moisture without more than normal watering.

Spread a 2-inch (5 cm) layer of peat on the soil and fork it in. Put a strong 5-foot (1·5 m) cane at each planting place (15–18 inches – 37–45 cm – apart). Push or hammer each cane about 18 inches (45 cm) into the ground, otherwise canes can lean awkwardly under the weight of a heavy truss of fruit later in the season.

Work in a normal dressing of a general fertilizer, rather than fuss about special fertilizers at this stage, and give the ground a reasonable watering if it is dry.

About the end of the first week in June, if you do not want to start your plants from seed, get plants which have been raised and properly hardened off by the nurseryman. You will probably have to take hardening on trust, as it takes a bit of experience to tell, except that if a plant has purplish dull, under-sized leaves you can bet it is not much use. Stand the plants, still in their pots, in their planting positions, but do not plant them. Just draw up soil to steady them. Give each pot a drink.

Next day, or later if you are busy, knock the plants out of their pots without root disturbance (or tear away the 'pots' if they are of soft plastic) and set each plant firmly into the ground beside its stake. If you prefer to plant them immediately you get them and cut out the delay, by all means go ahead. The drill described is not so much a final hardening as getting the plant accustomed to new surroundings. The move is a slight shock, and the transplanting is another slight shock. I have an old-fashioned idea that two gentle shocks on separate days are better than two together. I may be wrong.

The 'hardening-off' idea which has been mentioned means giving a plant a gradual change from its warm, glasshouse shelter to the cooler conditions of the open garden. Again it is a matter of avoiding shock, which, if the move is made suddenly overnight, can be serious enough to have a bad effect on the plant's ultimate growth and performance. A good nurseryman, like any good gardener who raises his own plants, spreads the 'hardening' process over two or three weeks, according to site and weather, so that the plant suffers no real shock at all.

The tomato plant needs to be tied to its stake at intervals as it grows. The commercial grower dodges this drill by growing the plant up a string and making plant and string spiral into one another by an occasional deft flick with the finger. But you with your plants and canes are left with a tying job. However, this is quick and simple if you use packs of ready-cut lengths of plant-ties. These are thin wire, covered with paper or plastic. Slip them round plant and stake, and twist the ends together. Don't strangle the plant: make the loop reasonably loose.

During their first couple of weeks, the plants need watering round their small root area to make sure they do not dry out. But over-watering should be avoided for two reasons: one is that it makes the ground cold and wet whereas tomatoes like warm soil; the other is that it will at least delay good rooting. Roots have a way of foraging and finding enough water where this is possible, but too-frequent watering discourages such foraging. It also tends to affect the near-surface soil more than the rest and you are liable to encourage formation of roots too near the surface, where natural water-supplies are at their poorest, instead of a little deeper where the moisture content is not so seriously affected by sudden changes of surface conditions.

Restrict growth to a single upright main stem. All the way up the stem there are leaf-stems, each with its neat group of leaves. Flower-stems also appear and are easily recognizable because their flower-buds show right at the start. But in the joints between leaf-stems and the main stem the plant produces side-shoots which, if left, would convert the plant into a bush. There are some varieties which can be grown successfully as bushes, but ignore them in what we are dealing with here. You must nip out side-shoots as soon as you see them. You should also buy a high-potash fertilizer such as Phostrogen or one specially formulated for tomatoes, and use this as directed.

If I have made the tomato sound like a crop that demands a great deal of attention, I suggest you re-read these few pages and you will find that I am merely trying to make it easy for you to understand a procedure which is neither tricky nor tiring. Nor is it time-consuming. However busy, or lacking in know-how you might think you are, you will be forever thankful if you try this crop.

Vegetable marrow. Although I find marrows no trouble to raise from seed (helped by a greenhouse) or to persuade into prolific production, my advice to the casual gardener would be to grow half a dozen plants and pick the marrows small. Indeed the trend is to grow small varieties, such as Custard Pie or to grow **Courgettes** which are like extremely small marrows and which make a tasty dish. The vegetable marrow variety Zucchini (a vigorous F^1 Hybrid) is highly suitable for growing as a courgette, that is, picking the marrows when they are only about 6 inches (15 cm) long. Sow seeds under protection and plant out in May, or sow outdoors in late May and early June.

Herbs are essential for every kitchen. How many you grow depends on your enthusiasm and I do not want to wish a load of work on to you. If you have a

Onion, All Rounder

sunny corner not too far from the kitchen you can sow short rows of sage, thyme, dill, chives, and parsley, if nothing more. Sow in March, and leave plenty of space for the sage because it can become a substantial bush. In addition, you ought to grow mint and perhaps horseradish because neither needs any care. They are, however, both extremely selfish, so keep them well apart from each other and well apart from other stuff whose ground they can invade. I grow them where their only scope to spread is into a grass pathway, where the mower keeps them under control.

Marrow (Green Bush, Gold Nuggett, Long Green Trailing)

Chives

Gherkin, Prolific

Pea, Early Onward

Kale, Dwarf Green Curled

Carrot, Nantes (Tip Top)

14 Pot Plants and Indoor Bulbs

Most plants grown in British homes die through drowning of the roots, and many of the remainder die of thirst when their owners are trying desperately to avoid drowning them. Drowning is usually effected by keeping the plant pot standing in a saucer of water to avoid parching. And parching usually happens when people think their plants are too wet. The pot dries out. Water is given, and it runs straight through and floods the saucer. The careful plant-lover throws away this surplus and stands the pot on a dry saucer, assuming that the plant has had enough water. He does not realize that the soil is full of air passages, due to dryness, and that it is down these air passages that the water has escaped past the shrunken particles of soil. It is a pity that Britain, which must be top of the European league for gardening, should be bottom of the league as regards interest in plants for inside the home. The chief trouble is this failure to understand watering. This in turn is probably due to lack of discrimination in choosing soil and pot.

In discussing plants for the home, let us be clear what range of plants we have in mind. The term 'indoor plant' covers any plant which spends its life indoors – or an important, though sometimes brief, part of that life. And the term 'indoors' covers anything from a dim room or chilly conservatory to an over-heated living-room. Since we are not concerned with time-consuming or expensive hobbies, we will deal with plants which are easy to look after and which will thrive in the home. The definition of 'house plant' has become blurred because some plants offered today as house plants serve only a short season under room conditions. Two examples are the poinsettia and the aphelandra. These are delightful plants during their period of colour. But to perform well for a second year they really need to go into a hot-house for a while. Calling these house plants gives the wrong impression that they qualify as permanent inhabitants of the living-room. Some plants which will grow in the open are used indoors to give a colourful display at a time when the weather outside would spoil their beauty. Bulbs such as hyacinths are an example. Others include annual flowers, such as schizanthus, which can be grown from seed and treated as temporary pot plants. Indoor plants for the home, therefore, comprise some which are worth their place all the year round and some which can be brought in for a short season. In both classes there are plenty of easy growers.

Having established the range of plants, let us now turn to the business of growing them. Once we have a plant, we must get the planting right, which we do by providing the right compost and the right pot. Failure in this causes root troubles and starts a vicious circle. Unhappy roots tend to rot and cease to take up moisture properly. This makes the plant droop, and gives the impression that it is too dry. But watering in this instance makes the problem worse and hastens the root-rot. And the plant soon dies. If soil and pot were right, there would be no guarantee that faulty watering would be eliminated, but at least the risk would be greatly reduced. At one time, clay pots were the only ones used – and I still use them for many purposes. They were favoured because, being porous, they reduced the risk of waterlogging – a risk made worse by the use of bad soil mixtures concocted by old-fashioned believers in muck and mystery. Development of scientifically balanced soil mixtures, by the John Innes researchers, changed all that and eliminated the need for stuffing the bottom of the pot with loads of old crocks to help drainage.

The John Innes mixtures include a seed compost, in which we sow seed, and three potting composts, known as Numbers 1, 2, and 3, for growing plants in pots. In the interests of easy gardening, we can forget all except Number 1 of these John Innes Potting Composts. Numbers 2 and 3 are physically the same as Number 1 but have stronger doses of plant food in them. If we use Number 1 for all purposes we can adjust the nutrient value by using liquid plant food occasionally. Numbers 2 and 3 are meant for enthusiasts who study plant needs carefully. The busy or casual gardener need not do this, as later feeding will correct the balance. For seed-sowing the potting compost may be a little rich, but it is only with tricky subjects that one need make that much fuss and we do not need to go in for any but the easy subjects. One difficulty is that John Innes composts are not always readily available. They comprise soil, peat, sand, chalk, and a fertilizer mixture. The soil (it is called 'loam') must have specific qualities if the physical balance is to be quite right, and supplies of the right soil are getting scarce. Also, the soil should be heat-treated (pasteurized) to destroy pests and weed seeds. Sometimes this is not done efficiently by those who mix and sell the composts, but I think we can take a chance. We want to enjoy our gardening rather than worry over these fine points. The great thing about the John Innes composts is the way they keep the roots happy. Peat serves as a spongy element to keep the roots moist. Sand (a hard, gritty sand) serves as an anti-binding agent to ensure that the peat does not clog tightly and squeeze out the small supply of air which is essential to root health. When you water a pot of John Innes compost, the peat acts like a blotter and absorbs moisture, while the surplus water flows down the drainage channels created by the coarse sand. I do not want to make this watering process sound perfect: it is not. If the compost becomes a little too dry the peat element does not immediately soak up enough of the water poured on to the surface. The surplus which drains down into the saucer should not be poured out immediately, but should be left for about half an hour to allow the soil to soak up its needs. After that time, empty the saucer, because a pot standing in water may ultimately become too wet, and short of air.

Instead of the John Innes compost, one can get some good composts based chiefly on peat. They are mostly referred to as 'soil-less' composts, and are excellent. But they have the disadvantage that if they get too dry – which can happen in the hands of busy people – they are difficult to re-wet. The best way to re-wet it is to stand the pot in a dish of water for a while. Even then, some of the dry peat floats off.

Some people find plastic pots easy to wipe clean, and since they are not porous, they do not dry out quickly in a warm, dry room. But they are also much lighter in weight than clay pots. And peat is lighter in weight than the John Innes composts. So a bushy plant growing in a peat compost in a plastic pot is liable to topple over as the compost dries. Whatever pot or compost you use, you are almost certain to start asking about the amount of water needed. There is a difference according to what plant you are growing, its stage of development, the season of year, and the room conditions. Although that may seem obvious, the question I am most

frequently asked concerning pot plants is: 'How often should they be watered?' Clearly, watering cannot be a matter of working to the clock. Feel the surface of the soil, and find whether or not it is moist. Don't just check one pot in a varied collection. Where you think water is needed, follow the drill I have described – give water, and leave for half an hour before emptying the surplus from the saucer.

Another saver of time and trouble is the self-watering pot. These pots are not really self-watering but they do hold a reserve of water which is released only slowly and enables the plant to go for much longer between waterings. They are twin pots, inner and outer, and there is a plastic foam fitting between the two. The plant is grown in the inner pot and water is poured into the space between this and its outer pot. The outer has an overflow hole in the side to ensure that water does not build up to too high a level. The inner pot takes up moisture only from the base, so it cannot flood. These pots take the guesswork out of watering and are ideal for those whose aim is easy gardening. All you need do is see that the reserve of water in the outer pot does not become exhausted.

There are other ways of making watering easier. One is to use one's own simple double-pot method. The smaller pot holding the plant is stood inside a larger pot and the space between the two is packed with moist peat (including the bottom of the outer pot). This method not only reduces moisture loss but also creates a moisture reserve which can be drawn upon by the inner pot, providing the peat is not allowed to dry out. Another method is to use a tray with a good layer of peat or sand on it. Keep the peat or sand constantly moist and keep the potted plants standing on it always. For these two methods to be most effective there should be no drainage material in the pot which holds the plant. Such material would insulate the compost from contact with the moist surface.

Positioning of pot plants in the room can make a difference to the ease with which they grow. Plants need light, some more than others, and can get distressed if short of light, especially in a very warm spot. But they do not want direct sunlight, which makes them sweat out moisture quicker than their roots can replace it, so that they flop. They also dislike draughts and such fumes as come from North Sea-gas appliances.

Early in this chapter brief mention was made of the fact that plants grown in the home comprise several categories. Perhaps we ought to run through them now and we can go into detail later. First, there are the true house plants, those which seem to survive for years even if sometimes neglected. Shrimp plant, Prayer plant, and Aluminium plant are examples. Cacti and succulents must be included in this grouping though they do need different treatments. Of the short-term plants, perhaps the most popular are bulbs, which are grown to bring indoors when in bloom, especially in winter and early spring. Then there are seasonal plants which we raise at home to give extra colour and variety temporarily. Some of these we raise from seed (schizanthus has been mentioned already) either in the home or in the greenhouse, specially to vary the house-plant display. More on this aspect is given in the next chapter (on the greenhouse). Some temporaries are what one might term florists' plants, which are usually bought in bloom from the florist. They fall into two sections. The first are those which are charming for one season but rarely do any good if kept for a second season under room conditions: aphelandra and poinsettia are examples. Next are those which, while giving a good display for a while, are not happy in room conditions all the year: the Indian Azalea is an example of this, and likes to be plunged outdoors for the summer.

Freesia, Choice Hybrids

It should be strongly emphasized that many greenhouse plants are eminently suitable for bringing indoors for a short spell when at their best and then for returning to the greenhouse when past their prime. Indoor fuchsias sometimes get upset and drop their blooms when brought into the living-room. But what matter? They can be taken back to the greenhouse. Try another fuchsia and it may stay happy. So please read this chapter in conjunction with the next one and use some greenhouse subjects in the home for short spells.

In the lists given later you may note some omissions, and you may wonder why, since some are easy. The fact is that I once loved them but now I dislike the very sight of them, largely because of the way they have been used. In case you like them, I had better name three popular ones. The first two are **Ficus Elastica** (rubber plant), and **Monstera Deliciosa** (Swiss cheese plant). These remind me of the foyers of big, over-heated, impersonal hotels. You will see them there. The third is **Sansevieria** trifasciata laurentii (known variously as Mother-in-Law's Tongue, Snake Plant, Bayonet Plant, and Bow String Hemp). It is a sub-succulent with long fleshy, sword-shaped, twisted leaves, mottled green and grey, with yellow edges. That should be enough to put you off it. I once almost liked it because it is so easy. But I tired of seeing it in almost every house window in Belgium, and later in much of the rest of Europe.

ALL-YEAR HOUSE PLANTS

Sufficient has been said about the permanent house plants for me to press on and start naming a selection. In doing so, may I be forgiven if I single out one for special treatment, partly because it has so many virtues, and partly because it has been a favourite of mine for many years.

It is **Clivia miniata**, an evergreen which produces gorgeous blooms in early spring. I have a score of them and I think every home should have at least one. It will probably come to you in a 5-inch (12 cm) pot and later, as it grows it will need moving on to a 7-inch (17 cm). It must never be hurried into a pot larger than it needs, because it prefers being pot-bound. A mature plant in a 7-inch pot has shiny, strap-like leaves which fan out gracefully. On the window of a flat, they would serve rather like a venetian blind, allowing you to see through them from close range but preventing a snooper across the road from seeing in. The flower-head is the size of half a football made up of a mass of 3-inch (7-cm) orange trumpets and is a spectacular sight. Keep it cool and fairly dry for two or three winter months, otherwise it will not bloom. I find that after its cool, dryish spell a plant brought into a warm room and watered carefully, quickly sends up a flower-spike. Here are other suggestions for your list of easy house plants, beginning with those which can stay in the home all the year.

Aralia. An evergreen with glossy leaves somewhat after the shape of fig leaves. I grew mine from seed, which is easy but slow. This slowness is a virtue because it means that the plant does not get out of hand, though I have seen it as a tall tree in Malta.

Begonia. Let us ignore for the moment the exotic, large-flowered, tuberous begonias and deal with the small-flowered fibrous-rooted begonias mostly derived from Semperflorens. They are well-behaved pot plants which go on flowering all through the summer and look attractive in all seasons.

Begonia Rex, with its colourful leaves, makes a good foliage plant. It is better if the growing-tip is pinched out to prevent the plant from getting leggy. It may also need discreet staking.

Beloperone Guttata (Shrimp Plant). To avoid its going leggy, keep it near the glass, at least till it is in bloom. Its so-called 'flowers' are bracts (modified leaves) which have the shape and colour of prawns (or shrimps).

Citrus sinensis (Sweet orange). A tolerant plant in all indoor conditions but prefers to be kept cool, airy, and in good light. A shrubby plant with glossy leaves. Scented blossom is followed by small (inedible) oranges.

Chlorophytum comosum variegatum. Known as the Spider Plant, and sometimes as St Bernard's Lily, it sends stems trailing downwards. New spidery plantlets form at intervals on these stems and are easily rooted. Leaves are striped cream and green.

Cyrtomium Falcatum (Holly Fern) is a handsome large fern which is leathery and almost indestructible. It is not fussy about where it is grown or what sort of soil it is given. The variety rochfordianum is rather smaller.

Impatiens (Busy Lizzie) is so easy that it is often neglected. Water freely in summer but not too much in winter. Flowers nearly all the year and flowers are mostly pink, also red, mauve, and white.

Ivy. There are ivies of various leaf size and some with variegated leaves. As pot plants they can be trained any desired shape by tying the stems to straight or hooped supports.

Maranta leuconeura. Has attractively marked leaves, in two shades of green which fold up like hands raised in prayer. Hence, it is often called the Prayer Plant, though an older name is the Arrowroot Plant.

Neoregelia carolinae tricolor. This is an epiphytic bromeliad which is easy to grow. It is a fun plant. The leaves make a big green rosette and the short ones in the centre form a red vase which should be kept filled with water.

Nerium oleander. A pink-flowered shrubby plant with dark, evergreen, willow-like leaves. It will grow outdoors in a sheltered situation in warm areas and can be stood outside for a while in summer after flowering.

Pelargonium (which is usually called **geranium**) I put among the permanent plants because it is happy indoors all the year and the foliage is pleasing. Cut it back fairly hard when it goes out of flower. The new shoots will spring from the cuts, and will flower.

Peperomia. Compact, bushy plants whose flowers are borne on spikes looking rather like rats' tails. Peperomia magnoliaefolia has pretty leaves with yellow margins.

Pilea cadierei nana (Aluminium Plant). Medium green leaves splashed with aluminium colouring. Nana is a dwarf variety which grows bushy naturally. The older variety may need pinching back to keep it bushy.

Pilea mollis is a lovely foliage plant of fairly recent introduction. It came to me unlabelled and I first thought it was a peperomia. That will give you a clue to its leaf type. The bi-coloured leaves are bobbly and wrinkled with charming maroon and green markings.

Tradescantia fluminensis. This is a trailer which will hide its pot, if some stems are shortened to make them multiply. The pale green leaves striped in white keep their stripes better in full light. If shoots appear with plain green leaves they should be removed.

Cineraria, Dwarf Large-Flowered Mixed

Hypoestes Sanguinolenta (Polka Dot Plant)

Next group of plants to consider, after those house plants which will serve all the year round, are the many items one can buy in pots at florists' shops. One must never be dogmatic in dividing indoor plants into separate categories, because the border-lines are too blurred. So-called 'florists' flowers' are sometimes kept in the home all the year, even though their bright display is short-lived. Some in this same category are often grown as greenhouse rather than as room plants. And similarly many plants recognized as greenhouse subjects (*see* next chapter) spend part of their life in the home – usually when at their most attractive. So in giving the following short list of useful 'florists' flowers' I am neither laying down the law nor suggesting rigid rules.

There are some florists' flowers whose dazzling beauty can turn quickly to disappointment in a living-room. Calceolaria, Cineraria, and Gloxinia are examples. Don't be afraid of them, but I am leaving them out of my list of easy subjects because they are liable to go floppy if your living-room conditions don't please them. If you grow them, give them a moist atmosphere. Do this by standing the pot on pebbles (just above the water-line) in a bowl of water. With all those points in mind I offer these few suggestions:

Aphelandra squarrosa Louisae (the Zebra Plant). The green leaves are boldly marked with white stripes along the veins. Its charm is a cockade of bright yellow bracts standing up in the middle. At the end of the season, throw it out or give it to a friend who has a heated greenhouse.

Astilbe (Spiraea). Likes a sunny spot but a moist atmosphere. Feathery plumes of flowers in red, pink, or white in spring. Transfer to open ground after flowering.

Azalea indica. This lovely little evergreen is usually bought in autumn or winter when it is in bud and it soon smothers itself with flowers. The plant remains attractive after the flowers fade. Plant it out in its pot for the summer, and lift it again for indoors in the autumn.

Begonia. The large-flowered hybrids are grown from tubers. Their double blooms are exotic but sometimes drop off in the dry atmosphere of the home. Keep moist air round them. They do well outdoors in summer, so plant them out if they are unhappy in pots.

Chrysanthemum. A florist's potted chrysanthemum usually comprises five plants in one pot, skilfully dwarfed and well furnished with blooms. It makes a colourful show. This is on sale at all seasons, thanks to the nurserymen's skill in light and heat control. If the plants are planted outside after flowering they will revert to tall habit and will flower in autumn.

Cyclamen persicum. It can be raised from seed (which takes skill) or bought as a plant. Keep it in a cool part of the room. Stand it on pebbles, in a bowl with water in the bottom. After flowering, the plant can be gradually dried off, kept somewhere cool, and restarted into growth the following season.

Euphorbia pulcherrima, better known as **Poinsettia**, is grown for its startling red bracts. Theoretically, if you dry it off after the bracts fade, cut it back hard in May, and restart it into growth then, you can get a second season of colourful display. But it is not easy. Better treat it as a one-season plant.

Saintpaulia (African Violet). Some say it is difficult but I have found it to thrive in a dry centrally-heated atmosphere. To be safe, give it the moist air treatment (pot standing in a bowl of moist gravel). It blooms for months, usually pretty blue shades, also pinks and white.

Succulents, Mixed

Solanum capsicastrum (Winter Cherry). An easy and popular subject with cherry-sized red berries which will stay on for a long time in a cool moist atmosphere.

CACTI AND SUCCULENTS

Whenever I come across the phrase: 'cacti and succulents', I think of a flower-girl in Newcastle upon Tyne who used to shout: 'Floo-ers or carnayshuns, hinney'. The word 'hinney' is a term of endearment, a dialect form of 'honey'. The rest meant: 'flowers or carnations', which implied that carnations are not flowers. Similarly, to speak of 'cacti and succulents' seems to overlook the fact that cacti *are* succulents. One should speak of them as 'cacti and *other* succulents'. All cacti are succulents but not all succulents are cacti. Doubtless, someone will want to remind me of an exception. The cactus Pereskia is not a succulent but is a leafy shrub. However, it is not in our lists and we can ignore it. The botanical difference between cacti and other succulents is chiefly that cacti have organs called 'areoles' in the leaf joints. That is a bit technical and not much help, so we need not worry about it. What we need to recognize is that there are two groups of cacti and other succulents – one group from the hot desert sands and the other from forest areas. Desert types are usually chubby with ends like chopped-off vegetable marrows, or they are like thick, hairy or spiky stems. They store large volumes of water to help them withstand long drought, hence their bulk. Two popular desert types are the Mammillarias (chubby in shape) and the Opuntias. One well-known Opuntia is the Prickly Pear, and I have tasted its fruits straight off the plant on the Maltese island of Gozo where the plants grow more than man-high. The fruit is pleasant and juicy but of no outstanding flavour. In this country, the Prickly Pear makes only a pot plant. I would describe the Opuntia as a collection of thick, green, prickly, oval biscuits butting on to each other. Of the forest cacti, perhaps the one we know best is the Christmas Cactus, which recently changed its name from Zygocactus to Schlumbergera. Its stems are made up of flattish, fleshy, oval sections joined together. At the tip of each stem it produces flowers, termed 'hose-in-hose types' because the flowers grow out of each other's centres like funnels joined together. A general rule with most cacti is that they want as much sunlight as possible in winter. The desert types should be kept almost dry (not dust dry) during that time because they rest then. But other types, such as the Christmas Cactus, may be in active growth in winter and will need careful watering. In summer, you will find that those which took a winter rest will come into active growth and will need regular watering. It is a mistake to think that a cactus which rests in winter will need water to bring it into new growth in spring. The plant will draw on its reserve store of moisture to start new growth.

Cacti are easy to raise from seed, so to start a collection you can buy plants or sow seeds according to how quickly you want results. You can get a great deal of fun and excitement out of raising a batch or two from seed. I have a friend who had no interest in cacti until his wife bought a packet of seed. From that beginning he developed an interest which took him right up to the presidency of one of the societies of cacti-growers and to the possession of two commercial-type greenhouses, filled with a collection worth several hundred pounds. In buying seeds, you will find you have a choice between the supremely easy and the normally easy. The supremely easy are the large-seeded ones such as Cereus and Opuntia. The more sophisticated, much smaller seeds, include such species as Echinocereus,

Ferocactus, and Mammillaria.

Compost for cacti is more important than many people imagine. It is quite wrong to think that cacti will grow in a bit of lifeless sand. They want a good compost, such as one of the John Innes mixtures, but they need to have it modified. You should mix one part of coarse, gritty sand to every two parts of normal potting compost so as to ensure a good open texture.

In choosing plants to make a small collection of cacti and other succulents, you should not trouble too much about full names or you may get lost in a realm which belongs to a group of specialist growers and enthusiasts. For instance, if you have an Opuntia, you should not try to sort out whether it is Platyopuntia, Tephrocactus, or Opuntia papyracantha. If ever the bug bites you or the spines sting you it will be different, but for the time being let us keep to easy gardening. And here I should like to give two warnings. First, regarding those with sharp spines. Do not have more of these than you can watch closely. They can be unkind to the flesh if they take you unawares. And on a window-sill they can get caught up in the curtains so that you swish the plant on to the floor as you try to let in, or shut out, the daylight. Next I warn you against a popular character called the Peanut Cactus (Chamaecereus silvestrii). It is an attractive subject but Red Spider mites also find it attractive and they are difficult to get rid of or to keep off your other plants. If you have a Peanut Cactus, put it outside by a sheltered wall and protect it with a sheet of glass in winter, but don't have it indoors. Apart from plants which I have mentioned already (mainly Mammillaria, Opuntia, and the Christmas Cactus) here are a few suggestions:

Aloe. Makes a rosette of thick, fleshy, pointed leaves. Flowers red, orange, or yellow. Aloe variegata is more colourful, in a darker green leaf with white markings. Trouble-free grower but is best repotted yearly in early autumn.

Aporocactus (Rat's Tail Cactus). The ribbed stems are long and trailing, hiding the pot. Flowers pink or red. Likes a rich, peaty soil.

Cereus. The flowers open at night. This is a large columnar plant with ribs which are spined or angular. An interesting subject.

Crassula argentea. A popular succulent, almost impossible to kill. The thick fleshy evergreen leaves grow big and lush if the plant is well fed. Flowers insignificant. Shoots snapped off will root readily. Overgrown plants will stand hard cutting back.

Echeveria retusa. Is happy in room conditions. Has the well-known rosettes of thick fleshy leaves and makes urn-shaped flowers in shades of red, orange, and yellow in spring or early summer.

Echinocereus. Another easy grower, with soft fleshy stems over a foot (30 cm) long and from 1 to 3 inches (2–7 cm) thick. Large flowers in white and shades of yellow, red, and purple in summer. Keep dry in winter.

Epiphyllum hybridum. I choose this from the many good epiphyllums. It is known as the Orchid Cactus and has large flowers, usually reddish, in spring and summer. Leaves are almost free from spines.

Gymnocalycium is an attractive globular cactus which likes to be well watered in summer. Likes semi-shade. Flowers are large, white or pink, in late spring or summer.

Lithops. Never fails to attract attention because the plant looks like a collection of pebbles. Virtually no water should be given in winter and careful watering is essential in summer. Flowers yellow or white in autumn.

Rebutia. This is a small, spiny plant and is one of the smallest of the cacti – usually about 2 inches (5 cm) across. Small flowers in a wide colour range are produced for a long period in spring and summer.

INDOOR BULBS

An absolute essential among plants for the home is to introduce a few bowls of bulbs, especially those to flower from Christmas into early spring. There is no hard work needed to grow bulbs in bowls or pots. Doubtless mistakes are made with them, such as giving too much water or too much heat at wrong times. But these mistakes are easy to avoid. In any event, you can buy bowls of bulbs ready to burst into flower, and they take no more looking after than a vase of cut blooms. For the busy gardener, I advise trying some of these ready-grown bulbs. You can also get dormant bulbs ready planted in containers so that they need no more than water to bring them into growth. Bulbs, therefore, must be classed as the easiest of temporary or seasonal subjects to help out the show of indoor plants.

Whether you buy them ready-planted or plant them yourself, it pays to know the do-it-yourself procedure if you want to get the best out of them. Hyacinths are probably the most popular indoor bulbs, and the procedure for them applies in large measure to that for growing other bulbs indoors. They are normally grown in bowls, which are obviously more decorative than pots. The difference between using pots and bowls is worth noting. A pot has a drainage hole and is suitable for soil (potting compost). This compost will nourish the bulb grown in it, so that the bulb will not only bloom but also will recharge itself ready to bloom the following season. Potting composts cannot be used satisfactorily in bulb-bowls because of lack of drainage. So bowls are filled with what is termed 'bulb fibre'. This fibre is a

Saintpaulia, Mixed

mixture of peat, oyster-shell grit, and charcoal. The peat serves as a sponge and root anchorage, while the other ingredients keep it sweet. But the fibre contains no nourishment. Therefore while the bulb, being a prepacked or embryo bloom, is able to flower, it gets no nourishment to help it recharge itself ready to bloom again the following season. The bulb ends up exhausted, but not dead. If it is then transferred to nourishing soil it will spend one blank season restoring its lost energies and will be ready to bloom again after that blank year. When I grow bulbs in fibre I plant them out after flowering. I put them in a warm border and leave them there permanently. That way, over the years, I have built up a lovely stock of hyacinths which give a great show outdoors every spring.

Now to the details of planting and raising bowls of hyacinths, to fill the room with scent and colour. The bulb fibre must be moist but not soggy. Moistening is tricky till you learn how. It is no good pouring water on to fibre and expecting to moisten it: the water will go to the bottom and the fibre will float quite dry on top. Put water in a bucket, put the fibre on top, and leave it for a day to soak up water slowly. If you have used too much water, you can gently press the fibre against the inside wall of the bucket and tilt the bucket to drain off the surplus water. When I plant hyacinths in bowls I like two-thirds of the bulb to be showing above the surface. Some people plant deeper but this means that the roots get less fibre. No matter how many bulbs go to a bowl, they should be all of one colour. They should be planted firmly but not packed too hard. Spacing should be such that they are close together but not touching. Large bulbs do better than small ones.

After planting, the bulbs must be kept cool and dark to encourage them to make roots before light or warmth tempts them to start shooting. Under the bed in a cold spare room will do. When an inch of growth is showing bring the bowl into full light, still keeping it as cool as possible. A big, strong root system is easier to

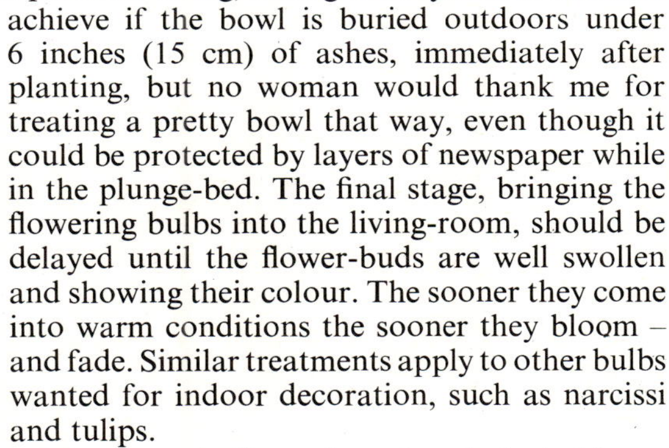

achieve if the bowl is buried outdoors under 6 inches (15 cm) of ashes, immediately after planting, but no woman would thank me for treating a pretty bowl that way, even though it could be protected by layers of newspaper while in the plunge-bed. The final stage, bringing the flowering bulbs into the living-room, should be delayed until the flower-buds are well swollen and showing their colour. The sooner they come into warm conditions the sooner they bloom – and fade. Similar treatments apply to other bulbs wanted for indoor decoration, such as narcissi and tulips.

Many people like to have hyacinths in bloom at Christmas. The way to do this is to make an early start – in September – and to use what are called 'specially prepared' bulbs. These bulbs have been subject to temperature manipulation so that first they ripened early, and then were held back. Once planted, they tend to hurry into bloom. With these prepared bulbs, it is wise to have all your planting equipment ready to enable you to plant them as soon as they reach you.

Thunbergia Alata, Mixed

Nowadays hyacinth bulbs are often sold by flower colour rather than by varietal name. If you want to be choosy, be guided by the details given in your catalogue and you will not be disappointed, provided you go for good size. A few names to look for are: Ostara, dark blue; Delft Blue, light blue; Jan Bos, crimson-red; Princess Irene, pink; City of Haarlem, yellow; and L'Innocence, white.

POT-PLANT PESTS

Pests are rare on most house plants but can be a menace if allowed to breed unnoticed. A few whitefly or greenfly may arrive on a bought-in plant and they breed rapidly. The first need is watchfulness. Glance at the plants while watering, and look at the undersides of the leaves. Spray *all* your plants with a good pesticide the moment you spot infestation.

I carry the plants outside and stand them in a straight row so that I can go right along the row with a systemic insecticide (*see* Chapter 17 for details about systemics and other pesticides).

When using pesticides, always read carefully every line of instruction on the label or on any leaflet issued with the bottle. Carelessness here can be harmful to the user. In addition, it can be harmful to plants, because you may find that a particular pesticide should not be used on certain plants because their leaves are oversensitive. Pyrethrum or derris will usually solve this problem.

Regarding whitefly, apart from getting rid of them, you might ask yourself why they are there, especially if they fly out in clouds whenever you touch a plant. Part of the answer may be that your plants are placed where the air is always too dry. Excessive dryness not only encourages whitefly, but makes some plants unhappy. It is not good to have plants standing on a shelf immediately over a hot radiator. Where plants have to live in such hot dry conditions, much trouble can be avoided by using a double-pot system or the sand- or peat-tray. These methods were described earlier in this chapter.

15 Greenhouse

You could be forgiven for imagining that a greenhouse has no place in the garden of anyone who aims at keeping his gardening chores to a minimum. But a greenhouse can be used any way you choose, and can be run in such a way as to give a greater return – in terms of value per minute – than any other part of the garden. You should see what a grape vine can do for you without hard labour or skill. Too many people think of a greenhouse as a place to give plants a good summer temperature most of the year. This is not correct. Most greenhouses are employed only to protect plants from extremes or rapid fluctuations of weather. The structure is meant to serve more as an umbrella or a screen than as a warming-room. Plants outdoors are liable to excesses of rain at certain times, and to cold winds. They are also subject to extremes of cold occasionally, including frost. For a vast range of plants the answer is not to put in heat but to keep out cold, while also regulating the availability of air and moisture. The greenhouse need not be heated and should certainly not be shut up without ventilation.

At one time I edited a greenhouse magazine which catered for enthusiasts. They got the maximum out of every square foot of glasshouse space. It involved skilful control of light, heat, and humidity, and those concerned grew a range of plants which would never have survived outdoors in this country. This needed time, skill, and equipment. But, apart from these enthusiasts, there are hundreds of thousands who use the greenhouse as no more than a shelter for plants some of which *could* grow outside but which do better through spending some or all of their time under a minimum of protection. I have mentioned the grape vine. It can be grown outside, but will produce earlier and bigger crops in the greenhouse. The emphasis here is on simple shelter without heating or coddling. Indeed, although the grape is such a delicious and rewarding crop, it is one of the least demanding. Far from crying out for heat, it thoroughly enjoys a good snap of frost in winter. That is the grape's only demand that I cannot satisfy. I cannot afford to give up the house entirely to a vine. Ninety per cent of the cubic area of the place is occupied by plants which ask only to be kept free from freezing. Not to be kept warm, mark you. It is merely freezing that would be damaging.

You may wonder why a vine occupies so little space or whether in that space it can produce worthwhile crops. Mine is a Black Hamburg and is planted *outside*. Its stem is led in through a hole in the wall at the end where the door is. The stem (technically called a 'rod') is led up the inside of the wall through a hole in the bench, and up to the top corner of the doorpost. The hole in the wall is large, to allow the rod to expand and is kept stuffed with straw. At the top corner of the doorpost the rod forks, having been trained that way, and becomes two instead of one. One rod goes straight along a roof support bar which runs the whole length of the building about $2\frac{1}{2}$ feet (75 cm) from the ridge-point or rooftop. The other rod, after going over the top of the door, runs along the support bar on the other half of the roof. From the time they grew into the prescribed shape and position, which took only three seasons, they have needed only simple pruning, and some strong ties without which the weight of the crop would pull down the rods. Apart from the fact that during summer the leaves give some useful shade, and that hanging bunches hit my head when I lean over the bench to water pot plants, one would not know that the vine was there.

Pruning could not be simpler. Fruiting shoots grow all along the rods at intervals of anything up to a foot (30 cm). In late December I cut every one of these down to a $\frac{1}{4}$ inch (6 mm) long, which leaves one little swelling (growth bud) from which the new shoot will grow in early spring. When spring growth begins, I rub off surplus shoots so as to leave only one shoot to grow every 9 or 12 inches (22 or 30 cm) along the rod. When the tiny bunch of blossom appears on the shoot, I trim off the end of the shoot at two pairs of leaves beyond that blossom truss. After that I keep snipping off surplus leaf growth. At all times I avoid coddling, and keep up maximum ventilation. I know of nothing simpler than growing grapes this way.

I hope your appetite has been whetted now, and that you see the greenhouse as an acceptable part of the easy-to-run garden. You need to consider many factors before you erect and plant up your greenhouse. Orthodox greenhouse gardening demands a fair amount of work, even though it is greatly rewarding.

The casual gardener can avoid it in either of two ways, by limiting his greenhouse activity or by using elaborate equipment for heating, ventilating, watering, and control of air humidity. The second method may increase involvement to the point where greenhouse gardening ceases to be relaxing. If the structure has walls of glass from floor upwards, one big chore, watering, can be reduced by plunging the plants in pots into the ground. Watering then can be done either by a trickle system, or manually by simply hosing the soil in which the pots are plunged. An occasional soaking of the border is usually enough except on the hottest days of the year. The reason why glass down to the ground is essential to this method of growing is that plants tend to reach for the light. If the lower part of the wall is of wood or other opaque substance, the plant will grow 'leggy' (that is, develop thin, weak stems) in seeking the light.

Please do not misunderstand me: I am not advocating a bench-less structure as the ideal. I am merely pointing out how it can simplify watering, which I find time-consuming in summer when benches are packed with plants. Benches are extremely useful, save bending, and can be equipped with trays of sand or peat so that much of the labour is taken out of watering. Indeed there are what are termed 'capillary benches' which keep the pots moist automatically.

Where pots are plunged into the greenhouse border, one thing to watch is that earthworms sometimes venture into a pot. Their presence is quickly detected by the expert because he promptly notices the plant's reaction, but the novice may find his plant suffering root disturbance, and not know the cause. I suggest precautions against worms at the start. You can treat the border soil with a worm-killer, such as chlordane, or cover the soil with a 4-inch (10 cm) layer of gravel or clinker, or do both.

Greenhouses can be obtained in various shapes and sizes, and the framework can be of metal or of a choice of timbers. One can have the glass down to ground-level or set up on a base – up to bench height – of wood, concrete, or brick. Rust-proof metal framework is expensive but durable. Timber varies in price according to quality and thickness, and its durability depends on which timber you choose and how well you look after it. There are several shapes, one of the least expensive being what is called the Dutch-light house, whose sides slope so that it is wider at the bottom than at the point where the roof begins. Get catalogues from several makers so that you can see what is available and choose according to your needs and your pocket. On the matter of size, be as generous to yourself as possible. The larger the house, the easier it is to avoid extreme changes of temperature, because a big volume of air obviously takes longer to heat up or cool down than does a small volume. But see that the size fits its chosen space without going too close to anything which might overshadow it. A glasshouse is intended to trap sun heat, not to sit in the shadow of a tall hedge. If aspect is right you might manage perfectly well with something built to lean against one of the existing walls of your home. Indeed, you could go further and make the glass structure an extension of the house, a sun lounge, which could be a greenhouse and extra living-room combined. Nor is glass the only material you can use for a suntrap: there are some good, safe plastics available.

Aerosol sprays are useful when the odd plant is found to have pests on it.

Young plants of Clivia miniata flowering well. As the plants mature the flower-heads grow bigger.

A point of argument concerns choice of direction in which to face the greenhouse. For the fair-weather gardener, the ridge running north–south has the advantage of giving a good distribution of light. It does not trap much warmth in midwinter when the sun sits low in the sky. Winter light may be vital to a commercial grower who wants to produce an extra early crop, but it does not matter much to the home gardener. Put the house where it will get what sun you can give it, but make sure it is convenient from all other aspects, including electricity and water-supply.

If ultimately you get bitten by that greenhouse bug which makes you want to warm the place in winter, the cheapest equipment is a self-feed paraffin heater. My glasshouse is fitted with electric heating controlled by thermostats. But in case of power cuts I also have a paraffin heater.

Lest you be misled, I must emphasize that much of the plant-raising activity which I shall be suggesting for the greenhouse can be done with simple equipment. Indeed, boxes of seedlings can be raised efficiently in what is termed the 'garden-frame', or under cloches, without the greenhouse, or in a small propagator. The garden-frame is a structure usually with sides of brick or wood and with a sloping lid of glass (the lid is called a 'light'). Apart from its role as a substitute for the greenhouse, it also helps the gardener who uses his greenhouse to raise tender or half-hardy plants for outdoors. He can use the frame in the 'hardening-off' process of preparing plants gradually to accept the change from greenhouse to open-air life.

Cloches can do the same job as the frame – and more. They have the extra advantage that they are easily movable so that they can be put over subjects growing anywhere in the garden and can be transferred from crop to crop as growth progress dictates.

I believe the name 'cloche', French for 'bell', originates from the fact that the first glass coverings used to protect plants in the open were bell-shaped jars. Cloches today are far from bell-shaped but the name has stuck.

The most efficient modern cloches are of rigid plastic, as protective as glass, but free from the constant risk of breakage. The latest and best of these adapts the principle of double glazing to hold in the warmth more effectively. It is a double wall of plastic designed to trap tubes of air between the two layers.

Now back to the greenhouse and to a point about its use in winter, even when no winter-flowering plants are grown in it. Many popular plants can be brought in and stored dormant over the winter. They include dahlias, chrysanthemums, gladioli, and tuberous begonias. The dahlias and gladioli can be stored dry while the chrysanthemums and begonias prefer to be in boxes of near-dry soil. Fuchsias and pelargoniums brought in for the winter can be left in their pots with their stems cut short, and kept near dry till ready to wake up in spring. Even in midwinter you should allow ample ventilation. Only when it is necessary to lock out frost should you have door and ventilators closed.

Gladioli and begonia tubers can be kept dormant till ready for planting outdoors, gladioli till April and begonias till late May. But enthusiasts will start the begonias into growth in boxes of peat indoors for earlier results. Busy people need not do this, nor need they worry about taking cuttings of dahlias and chrysanthemums as is normally done. Dahlia roots can be left till planting-out time in April.

Chrysanthemums should have the soil in the boxes slightly moistened occasionally, and by March you should see signs of new growth. The easy way then is to cut away bits of old stem, even if new growth is on them, and keep only the shoots which are springing from the roots. These growths should have the tops pinched out to keep them short and bushy. The boxes should go outside in late April/May into a frame, or under cloches, or against a sheltered wall, where they can learn gradually to live outside. In May you can empty the boxes, and if you gently ease the green shoots away from the old roots you will find that you have self-made cuttings. (For reasons I do not know, these self-rooted plants are called 'Irishman's Cuttings'.) Plant them out, or as many of them as you want to grow, and they will replace the ones you dug up the previous year. So you see, you don't need the skill that chrysanthemum enthusiasts might tell you is needed; though, mind you, they get up to lots of clever tricks to produce those magnificent big blooms which they grow for shows.

Those potted fuchsias and geraniums which should have been cut down to about 3 inches (7 cm) when you brought them indoors will need to have their soil gradually moistened from February. By March you should see plenty of new growth. Pinch back shoots that get too long. You need not worry about hardening them off if you are not planting them out before mid-June. By then, if the greenhouse is being kept well aired, and if the weather is reasonable, they can be moved out without suffering any shock.

Most plants described as 'geraniums' are pelargoniums. There is no need for you to worry about names of varieties, as you might do with roses, because all are extremely easy to grow and you should buy the plants whose flowers appeal to you. The Regal and Zonal pelargoniums both make bushy plants but the Regals have larger flowers. All pelargoniums can be kept bushy if you nip out the growing-tip of every shoot till the plant is the size you want. Nip out the tip while the shoot is still short, just long enough to be showing its third pair of leaves. What happens then is that two shoots grow out to replace the one you nipped. This process, called 'bi-furcation', is carried out with care and skill by specialists to produce prize-winning plants. But you can make an attractive enough plant doing it your own casual way. Some young plants are sold, in flower, without having had proper shaping. Don't blame the nurseryman too much for this. A well-grown bushy plant takes time and space to grow, and becomes expensive. The public doesn't appreciate this and so there is not much sale for larger plants. People, not unnaturally, also want to see what sort of flowers the plant will give, so they are happy to buy a plant which has been allowed to flower too soon. But the result is that the plant may grow tall and leggy rather than bushy. The remedy is to be ruthless. Snip the plant down to a leaf joint 3 or 4 inches (7 or 10 cm) from the base. It will then grow two new shoots, which again should be nipped out when their third pair of leaves begin to show. Soon you will have four shoots and these in turn should be given the nipping-out treatment. To summarize, you nip out each growing tip so that the shoot becomes two, and you keep on doing that till the plant is big enough and bushy enough. The plant will be in bloom six to eight weeks after the final pinching out.

With your potted pelargoniums or geraniums you have several choices: you can plant them outside for the summer; you can leave them in the greenhouse; you can use them in the home while they are in bloom and then take them back to the greenhouse; or you can keep them all the time in the house. I use some as house plants, but prune them hard and put them back into the greenhouse when they begin to look short of flowers.

Fuchsias can be given the same sort of treatment as described for pelargoniums, but some of them drop their flowers when brought into a dry room.

When you start going beyond subjects such as those already mentioned you may be straying outside the realm of casual gardening, but you may well find it worth while and it is certainly not difficult. Without committing yourself you could give a thought to the perennials mentioned in Chapter 5; some of the outdoor bulbs in Chapter 7; the annuals (especially the half-hardies) in Chapter 9; and the indoor plants in Chapter 14. You could also think of giving an early indoor start to some of the vegetables mentioned in Chapter 13. Indoor sowing hints are given in Chapter 16 on propagation.

In the short list of selections which follows will be found some that have been referred to in the chapters mentioned, but the listing here is not a duplication. It is a reference to varieties of special interest.

Cineraria, Brilliant Mixed. This is a good mixture in pinks, scarlets, and blues,

Two plants just knocked out of their pots to show the state of their roots. It can be seen that one is a mass of roots, being overdue for potting on into a larger pot while the other is just at the right stage for repotting.

Plants from previous picture, having come from 3-inch (7 cm) pots, are ready to go into the 5-inch (12 cm) pots shown here. The picture illustrates an easy modern method of pot drainage. A small disc of perforated zinc is in place over the drainage hole and a little moist peat is ready to drop in before the potting compost is placed in the pot.

with white circles in them. A biennial, and not an easy subject, but has brilliant daisy-like flowers and large leaves. Requires shade. Sow under glass in April/May, and pot up finally into 6-inch (15-cm) pots. Bring them in as house plants in winter.

Coleus, Rainbow Mixed. A foliage plant with a wide range of mixed-coloured leaves in variations through pale green, pinks, and reds to chocolate-brown. Flowers are insignificant and should be nipped off to help the plant.

Ferns. Good pot plants for the house. Perhaps the best known is the Maidenhair Fern. Sow the spores on the surface of the compost, cover with glass, and stand the pot in a saucer of water to keep moist.

Freesia, Choice Hybrids. Their scent is wonderful and they do best if adequately supported from the start by thin canes. The seedlings grow into small bulbs which can be dried off for replanting the following year.

Gerbera, Jamesonii Hybrids. Daisy-like flowers large and colourful, which are good for cutting. Colours are delicate shades of primrose, apricot, pink, and scarlet. Needs no heat and will grow outdoors in a sheltered spot in warm areas.

Grevillea robusta. Sometimes used in outdoor displays but is excellent when grown in pots as an indoor foliage plant. It has graceful, silky, fern-like leaves.

Hypoestes (Polka Dot Plant). An unusual house plant with dark green leaves covered in pink spots. Looks especially good under electric light, and is easy to grow.

Impatiens Dwarf Mixed. Busy Lizzies are mentioned in the house-plant list. This is a dwarf, 6–9 inches (15–22 cm) in shades of pink, carmine, scarlet, and orange besides white. Although perennial, it is best raised afresh from seed each year.

Ornamental Pepper. These are dwarf types of capsicum, with brilliant little red fruits, some round and some conical.

Primula. There are three popular primulas for pot work – obconica, malacoides, and sinensis – with several varieties of each. All like cool shady conditions but can be brought into the living-room when buds start to open.

Mimosa pudica. Some people call this the Sensitive Plant. I call it the Humble Plant. But regardless of that, it is a fun plant whose dainty fern-like leaves curl at the slightest touch. They soon recover ready to repeat their trick.

Thunbergia Alata Mixed (Black-Eyed Susan) is a climber which you can train up a tall cane or any other support in the greenhouse to give a touch of the unusual to whatever sort of display you make of your greenhouse collection.

Finally, though mention has been made already of the wide range of non-greenhouse subjects which can be started or helped along in the greenhouse, there are two perennials which warrant special mention for greenhouse sowing. One is a polyanthus mixture whose seeds are in pellet form. Raise the plants and put them outdoors in a shady border. The other is Pansy Prize Mixed, which does exceptionally well if treated as a half-hardy annual. That means sowing the seeds indoors in February or March.

16 Propagation

The subject of propagation is not one for intense study by the casual gardener because he can save time by buying the plants he needs rather than troubling to raise them for himself. But there are exceptions. Some subjects are easier to grow by sowing the seed than by setting out plants. Some are so incredibly easy that it would be folly to think that time could be saved by buying in. Some propagation is fun rather than work. And, finally, some simple propagations can save money on a scale out of proportion to the effort involved. This is especially so when one is trying to plant a garden from scratch – and the bigger the garden the more it applies.

Broadly, propagation means multiplying plants; making several grow where only one grew before. The chief method is by sowing seed but there are several other methods, some quite fascinating. Sometimes propagation is subsidiary to cultivation. For example, when you sow a row of lettuce seed because you want to grow something to eat, that is clearly cultivation. If you sowed the lettuce just to make the plants produce seed to help grow more and more lettuce you might say that was strictly an exercise in propagation. But these are merely differences of aim. Lest there be any confusion, this chapter deals with all plant propagation, whether the aim be to consume the crop as soon as ready or whether it be to enjoy having the plants decorate the garden, temporarily or permanently. The essential difference between the treatment of the subject here, and some things you may learn elsewhere about propagation, is that we are looking mainly at the easy subjects and the easy way of propagating them.

It is not proposed to skimp the subject of seed-sowing, especially since this has been acknowledged as the most common method of propagation. But since you can get a great deal of help from your catalogue and the individual seed packets, let us leave that method till last. We can deal first with propagation methods which are least understood and often wrongly believed to be difficult.

The simplest of all is what is called *dividing*. Not only is it easy, but at times it becomes essential. Without it, plants can grow into over-large clumps and run into the various troubles overcrowding creates. How you divide depends on the type of root system, but you need not worry about that. A plant (other than a shrub) which had perhaps two or three shoots at the time you planted it and has now become a dense cluster of countless shoots wants dividing. Such plants have stems which die in winter to be replaced in spring by new ones from the ground. They include some bulbous subjects and some we call 'hardy border plants' or 'hardy herbaceous perennials'.

Do not try to memorize finer points about which plants like to be divided in autumn and which in spring. A rough guide is that an early-flowering subject dislikes spring disturbance because the time is too near its flowering season. But it does not much matter. And anyhow, on a heavy, cold soil, spring disturbance can be a safer bet, whatever the subject. Just dig up your overgrown clump in

March and stand it on a large sheet of brown paper or sacking. Pull the soil away gently so that you can examine the root structure. You will find that some roots can be torn up like a piece of turf if you take a firm grip on them and do a bit of tugging. Bulbous root systems will fall apart without much effort. Some roots might be so tough that they need chopping with a spade, though purists would raise their hands in horror at such a suggestion. If you do need to chop a root, trim off with secateurs any damaged pieces, and dust the cut surfaces with lime. Whatever method you use, the divided portions should each be given as much space as the original clump. And that might mean giving some of the root to a neighbour or throwing some away.

Another system of propagating is termed *layering*, which is started during the active growing season. There are two ways of doing this but one of them, air layering, is more for the enthusiast than for the busy or casual gardener. It involves slitting a stem, covering the slit with a ball of moist material such as moss, wrapping the moss-ball in polythene and securing it so that the moisture does not evaporate. After rooting has been achieved the upper part of the stem, complete with root system, is removed and potted up. The second method is simpler, especially where pliable or low-growing stems can be pegged down on the ground. When I use this method, I make a slit in the stem at the point where it will conveniently make ground contact. I slip in a piece of match-stick to keep the slit from closing. Then I peg down the shoot with a U-shaped piece of stout wire, heap some soil over it, and tie the tip of the shoot, in an upright position, to a cane. The virtue of layering is that while we are waiting for new roots to form at the slit, the mother plant's root system helps to sustain the shoot. The disadvantage of this procedure for the casual gardener is that it takes time, during which the layered shoot is vulnerable to anyone who is careless with feet, hoe, or herbicide.

Layering, like seeding, occurs naturally with some plants. An example of natural tip-layering is seen in the blackberry. Long shoots reach out and bend downwards till their tips touch the ground. Roots form at the tips (hence the term 'tip-layering') and a new plant springs up from these roots. Thus one finds long, strong stems rooted at both ends. The stems continue to multiply and to root at their tips until they form that impenetrable entanglement which we call the bramble patch.

If you look at a strawberry bed, you will find that the plants have a characteristic not unlike that of the blackberry. Long thin shoots grow out from each plant and little plantlets form at points along the shoots. When these plantlets make contact with the soil they quickly take root.

By taking note of these natural habits, one can learn a great deal about plant propagation. What some plants do naturally, others can be persuaded to do with a little help. Plants with long flexible stems are easily propagated by layering, as soon as a stem is long enough to be pegged to the ground and partly covered with some soil in which to root.

ROOTING CUTTINGS

The method I advise busy people to use for shrub propagation is to *strike cuttings*. This is not strictly one method but two, because nearly all shrubs can be grown from hardwood cuttings taken in autumn, and many can be propagated from what are termed 'softwood' cuttings, in summer. The summer cuttings can

Placing drainage material in the bottom of the seed-tray

Placing sowing compost in seed-tray

Using a board to firm the compost

Immersing trays in water to moisten the compost

Sifting compost over the sown seeds to cover them

Covering the seeds with glass and paper to keep in moisture and keep out light

be more fun but the autumn cuttings are the easier. Taking hardwood cuttings in autumn is so simple that one might almost describe it as just a matter of popping the cutting into the ground, leaving it, and waiting to see what happens the following spring. Of course it is not quite that easy, but you may have heard stories of people who have planted something very carefully, put in a stake to support it, and then found that the plant died but the stake took root and flourished. The story has gone the rounds for so long that I have never been able to trace the source but I *have* known stakes take root. Some of the willows root so easily that if you casually stick them in as stakes they are liable to grow. Bits of willow that I have used as small stakes have done that. Moreover I know a nursery which stopped selling at least one willow, the orange-barked Dutch Osier (Salix vitellina), because it is too easy to bother with. Instead, they sell you unrooted cuttings and tell you just to stick them in the ground and let them root themselves.

At the other extreme are specialists who recognize the need for the utmost care over choice of material for rooting some subjects. These specialists do a grand job because their skill in every aspect of production ensures nearly 100 per cent rooting success and consequently a lower price to the buyer of the plant. But bear in mind that you do not need 100 per cent success with the bits of twig you try to root. You are more interested in finding the quick and easy way.

First, look at the problem. A leafless shoot in late autumn or winter is at rest, and stays at rest until the rising temperature and lengthening days of spring urge it to swell its buds. That bud-swelling needs the help of a sap-flow, supported by roots which extract moisture from the ground. If you cut off that resting shoot in late autumn, and keep it in reasonable conditions, it will first try to skin over the cut end (what is termed 'forming a callus') and next it will feel the urge to seek moisture ready to meet the spring demand for sap to swell the bud. And its answer to that urge is to start making its own root system. Being able to see the problem and to know how the cutting reacts to it, we have to meet the point mentioned in the previous paragraph about the cutting's need for 'reasonable conditions'. Conditions must not be so wet that the cutting will rot, nor so dry that it will shrivel up, nor so cold that it will freeze, nor so warm that it sweats. This calls for a slightly moist, well-drained, cool position, with the bottom end of the shoot far enough below the surface to be reasonably safe from normal frost spells. (Frost does not often worry plant life that is 3 or 4 inches (7 or 9 cm) below the surface in well-drained ground.)

My answer is to choose a sheltered part of the garden, make a V-shaped slit in the ground by pushing in a spade and levering it a little, line the slit with sand, and stick the cutting into the slit. I use the spade again to lever the soil back firmly against the cutting and then tread along the line of cuttings, using my weight and my boots to firm the ground. The V-shaped drill should be a straight line, and a length of string helps to guide us in the initial spadework.

The cutting itself is important, even though we do not have to worry about the precision which so much concerns the specialist. The cutting must be firm and ripe, not soft; and should be healthy, which means showing no nasty discolorations or signs of injury. It is difficult to explain to the inexperienced that despite all this, one can do better with what is called 'young wood'. Young in this sense does not mean the last few inches of growth made by the plant. Rather might it mean (since the wood must be ripe) the *first* part of a shoot which began to grow in the spring of the year in which we are taking the cutting. This is not terribly critical, but the beginner should try to avoid using either wood from the previous year's growth or soft tips of shoots which grew out in late summer. The specialist might know how to make good use of either, but then he is a specialist.

Length of cutting has not been specified because there can be considerable variation – say from 4 to 12 inches or 10 to 30 cm – and experience is needed to ensure the right decision. Do not be afraid to try your judgment according to the advice already given about choosing the wood in the right condition. Where in doubt, an easy answer is to try several cuttings of differing lengths for each subject. They can't all go wrong. How deep to insert the cutting depends on its length. I should say not less than two-thirds of the cutting should be below the soil surface, and preferably three-quarters.

Don't rush impatiently to pull up your cuttings in spring to see whether they have rooted. Just stand back and admire them and leave them alone. And don't let your admiration carry you away too soon. Cuttings sometimes burst into life and look a great success when they are living only on the reserve that was in the wood when you cut it, and have failed to make any root at all. Pull out the ones that have gone dead and black, but leave the rest till the following autumn, when they will be ready for planting wherever you want them.

Softwood (or summer) cuttings need a different technique; not really difficult, but different; and it can be good fun. As we did with the hardwood late autumn cutting, let us look first at the problem. The shoot while it is on the plant is growing, is full of leaf, and is discharging moisture into the air through those leaves. It is also breathing through them, and is completely dependent on the root system to extract enough moisture from the ground to maintain the sap-flow. The moment you snip off the cutting it is like a ship in mid-ocean whose engines have broken down. It has to drift, helped only by the currents and the skill of the helmsman, until the engines can be got going.

That is a situation which cannot go on for long without serious trouble (whether you think of the ship or of the cutting). In the case of the cutting the first job is to reduce the natural moisture loss through the leaves, since we know we cannot properly replace that loss till we persuade nature to provide a new rooting system. There are two ways of doing this and we must use both. One is to remove what leaves we can spare (say all bar the top pair) and the other is to shut up the cutting in a small volume of moist air, since we know that things do not dry out if the air round them is as moist as they are. Also, since time is not on our side, we must encourage the cutting to make its root quickly – in a matter of days rather than months. If 'days' sounds an exaggeration let us aim at about three weeks. The aids to speed are warmth, good drainage, and hunger in the soil. The hungry, comparatively dry soil will challenge the cutting to find water by rooting and foraging. Unfortunately, the same warmth can cause fatal moisture loss if we do not keep the cutting well sealed. On the other hand, a completely sealed, moist atmosphere can cause other worries, so perhaps a daily change of air will help.

My grandmother had a simple way of solving all this, without ever thinking of it as a tricky or technical problem. She just stuck cuttings (slips or snippings, she called them) into sandy soil in a shady part of the open garden and plonked a jam-jar upside-down over the top. She did nothing more till the cuttings had rooted, which they did, and then she removed the jar and left them to get on growing till she was ready to plant them out or give them away. I suppose you will say she had green fingers. I know that the so-called 'sandy' soil was in a corner where she had worked in a couple of buckets of sand to help lighten the natural soil.

Choosing the right shoots for a summer cutting is no more difficult than choosing hardwood cuttings, though again it is different. The cutting should preferably come from a side-shoot and should be what is termed 'half-ripe' rather than lush and floppy. The test for 'half-ripe' is to lay the cutting across your fingers, inside the hand, and then bend it by pressing down with the thumb while tending to close the fingers. Some say that if the shoot is ripe enough it should snap. Perhaps if the bending is done in a slick movement, ripe wood will snap under that test. But my way is to press gently and I like to see the wood bend, reluctantly, then spring back straight again when I release the pressure. If the shoot stays bent when released, I rate it too floppy, too soft for striking.

Striking should be done in a good modern cuttings compost of which several proprietary brands are on the market. Some are multi-purpose composts suitable for cuttings and other work. Stick the cuttings round the inside rim of the pot of compost. Use cuttings about 3 inches (7 cm) long but don't be too hidebound about length. Remove all but the top pair of leaves and put the cutting two-thirds of its length into the compost. The bottom of the cutting preferably should end just below a leaf-joint. Moisten the soil, then slip a plastic bag over the pot, secure with an elastic band. Remove the bag daily and turn it inside out to prevent accumulation of excess moisture. Keep your pots of cuttings in the shade till rooting starts. Fuchsia and pelargonium cuttings taken in late summer and autumn should *not* be covered.

In both these matters of softwood and of hardwood cuttings I have heard people, as experienced as myself, declare that hormone rooting powders are unnecessary. By the same token, my grandfather swore that safety-razors were not as good as cut-throats. Yes, I can strike cuttings without using hormone rooting powders. But I always use them unless I am in too big a hurry. I use them because they speed rooting, especially of temperamental items. And I certainly advise all but the greatly experienced or truly green-fingered to use them. Some of these rooting powders are specifically for hardwood (autumn) cuttings and some for softwood (summer) cuttings. If you are buying a powder with such limitations, be sure you get the one suited for the job you want to do.

There are other easy tricks with cuttings in pots. For instance, instead of enclosing the pot in a plastic bag, you can just stand it inside a larger container and cover this with a sheet of glass. You should put an inch of moist peat in the larger container which should preferably be a plastic pot. A clay pot will do, but being porous it lets moisture escape. When you stand your pot of cuttings inside the bigger pot there should be an inch (2·5 cm) of space left between the top of the small pot and the rim of the larger. The space can be bigger if necessary, but don't use anything too large or you might find it difficult to prevent the air inside it from drying out. After covering the outer container with its sheet of glass, put it in the shade. Moisture will form on the inside of the glass and if there is too much it will drop on to the cuttings and might make them go mouldy. That is why with the plastic-bag procedure you are advised to turn the bag inside out occasionally. The double pot and sheet of glass are less bother, because the glass merely has to be turned over each day.

Another work-saving drill which I employ with some slow-rooting evergreen cuttings again involves using two pots, but I use no glass covering. I use clay pots, a 6-inch (15-cm) and a 3-inch (7-cm). First I put enough moist peat in the larger

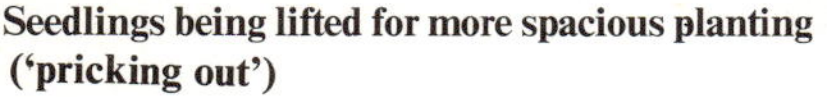

Seedlings being lifted for more spacious planting ('pricking out')

The seedlings pricked out and placed evenly in another seed-tray

pot to ensure that when the small pot is stood inside, the brims of the two pots are about level. Then I pack the space between the two pots with rooting compost. It is in this space, between the walls of the two pots, that I stick the cuttings. I put the double pot in the shade and check occasionally to see whether the compost is getting too dry. If it is, I just put water into the empty small pot in the middle. When top growth indicates that the cuttings are well rooted I pot them up singly in the normal way.

Another method of propagation which nurserymen employ outdoors with some subjects is termed *stooling*. Briefly this means cutting the plant short, covering it with a hummock of soil, and waiting for new shoots to grow on the hummock. These shoots are found to have their own root system so they can be dug up and transplanted singly. I have already in Chapter 5 described a modified form of this system for heather. You smother a clump of heather with a mixture of half sand and half peat in spring and the heather roots in it and grows through it. This is not the only easy way to increase heather; short cuttings taken in July or August will root quickly in pots of rooting compost.

SEED-SOWING

It was indicated at the start of this chapter that seed-sowing – the most common of all methods of plant propagation – was being left till last. General hints on the subject had been given already in Chapter 9, on hardy and half-hardy annuals, and in Chapter 15, on greenhouse gardening. If we now look at seed-sowing as an essential aspect of plant propagation and treat it in greater depth, it will help us to see different sowing techniques in better perspective and perhaps underline points of procedure which, though they seemed insignificant, can make the difference between success and failure.

Every good seed firm offers guidance in its catalogue or on the seed packet, or both. It is generally acknowledged that the most comprehensive information offered on any seed packet is that given by Carters, whose packets have been completely and expertly redesigned in recent years.

However, there are always some people who do not read instructions carefully and some who misinterpret them. It is useful, therefore, to consider general principles of plant-raising from seed and to clarify or emphasize a few points. Failure with seed-sowing is sometimes due to carelessness either in the way the seed has been handled in the home or by failure to follow simple directions. It is often due to impatience; to an anxiety to get going before the soil and weather are right. People who suffer disappointments frequently express amazement at the way self-sown seedlings thrive under seemingly impossible conditions. But nature scatters her seeds by the million and only a tiny percentage succeed. The worst of gardeners has a bigger percentage of success than nature ever had. So take heart. All the same, we have learned a vast amount from nature by studying her types of seed and her methods of distribution. The seedsman applies this knowledge in producing, harvesting, and storing seed, and in giving directions to the gardener on how to get the best results. Everything from breeding to selling is done with specialist knowledge, and that is why the sower can hardly go wrong unless he ignores what he is told.

I store dry packets of seed in large airtight tins from the moment they are received and checked. The reason for using more than one tin, is to separate vegetables from flower-seeds and to sort the flower-seeds into their various categories. The tins are kept in a cool, dry store. The result is that the seeds do not suffer from dampness or drying-out. When seed is used from a packet, the packet is promptly resealed with transparent sticky tape and put back into the tin.

With outdoor sowings, the date of sowing indicated by the seedsman is only a rough guide. How close you stick to that guide depends on soil and weather. But don't be tempted to sow ahead of the suggested date just because conditions seem right. Do not let a false spring tempt you to do March sowings in early February, for example. Directions for vegetable seeds sometimes indicate an extended period for sowing. This usually means that you should make several sowings at intervals, and not sow too many at a time.

Where depth of sowing is not specified, it may be making allowance for different types of soil. For example '2 to 3 inches' is an attempt to indicate minimum depth (for heavy soils) and maximum depth (for light soils). There are exceptions to all the general rules about soil conditions, but where these occur they are clearly stated in the catalogue or on the packet. Seed likes soil to be fine and crumbly, warm and moist, and after sowing, it likes the soil firm but not bone-hard. The gardener's job in helping to provide these conditions is to work the soil into its crumbly yet firm state by breaking it up well, allowing it time to settle, and raking the surface thoroughly. The ideal crumbly state referred to is termed a 'good

Pelleted seed can be evenly and carefully spaced at sowing time so that no pricking out will be needed

On the left is a tray of plants from pelleted seed while on the right are plants from non-pelleted and these will need pricking out

tilth' in gardeners' and farmers' jargon, but more is still needed for success. The soil should be moist but not wet, which means that there should be a reasonable amount of moisture *in* the ground but it should not be sitting on the surface. Temperature also should be right for the time of year or certainly not substantially below it. Weather news is plentiful these days and daily reports usually indicate how far the temperature is from the seasonal normal.

In outdoor conditions, $\frac{1}{4}$ inch (6 mm) is about right as the sowing depth for small seeds. Bigger seeds, such as peas for instance, can be sown as deep as 2 inches (5 cm). Two common causes of failure with small seeds are sowing them too deeply and sowing them too close together. If seeds are nearly touching the plants will choke one another and be a failure. After sowing, and covering with the right amount of soil, the seeds should be made firm by gently hitting the ground all along the row with the shoulder of the rake. As the seedlings come through, they should be thinned, which means removing the surplus to leave the remainder enough room to develop. The thinning can be done in stages, and with plants which have to stand a foot and more apart, that is the general practice so as to allow for casualties.

A great deal of sowing is not done in the final rows but in seedbeds. Here, the rows are shorter, closer together, and the thinning done is only the amount needed to allow the plants to reach a suitable size for transplanting to their final quarters. Where there is any doubt about the adequacy of the soil moisture when sowings are being planned, any soaking required should be done in advance rather than after sowing. Watering disturbs the soil and it is also liable to batter down the soil and destroy its firm crumbly surface. Water afterwards if you must, such as when total lack of rain is obviously leaving the seeds too dry in the soil. But it is better if you can avoid it.

COMPOST FOR SOWING

Sowing *indoors* is a different technique from sowing outdoors. Indoors, for instance (except for such things as peas and beans) I cover seeds very lightly. The depth of compost put over them is rarely more than the thickness of the seed.

May I remind you again of our mnemonic PEP which we coined to remind us of the constant need to have our pattern of operation, our equipment, and our plants in harmony with each other and in keeping with our needs. For indoor sowing, emphasis is on correct equipment. Slap-happy sowing, using the wrong equipment and materials, causes not only failures but pest and disease troubles, which can affect all the occupants of the greenhouse, frame, or cloche in which the sowings are to germinate.

Old-type wooden seed-trays are still good if kept clean, but plastic seed-trays are easier to clean, easier to handle, and longer lasting. They usually have adequate drainage holes and apart from putting a little coarse peat in the bottom, no special drainage precaution is necessary before filling up with modern composts. You can get peat-based general-purpose composts, such as Cuthberts All-Purpose Sowing and Potting Compost to save having several bags or heaps of different composts. If you are working on a small scale, and you prefer the John Innes soil-based types, you can, as I previously mentioned, stick to the Number 1 Potting Compost, and you could put crocks in the bottom of the tray for drainage.

Compost must be moist but not wet before it is put into the trays or pots (I use pots for small sowings, such as of shrubs) so that it can be made firm without

Some seedlings are moved into separate pots, so that later moves can be made without root disturbance. This picture shows how tomato seedlings are potted early to the full depth of their stems so that the seedling leaves rest on the surface. If planted to the same depth as they stood on the trays in which they had been raised from seed, they would tend to be leggy, that is, too long and thin of stem.

These are rooted cuttings of a house plant, Pilea mollis, ready to be moved into separate small pots.

Inexperienced growers can fail with cuttings either by over-watering, which causes the cuttings to rot, or by under-watering, which allows them to flop. An easy answer is the two-pot method. A 3-inch (7-cm) pot is placed inside a 6-inch (15-cm) pot and the space between is filled with compost.

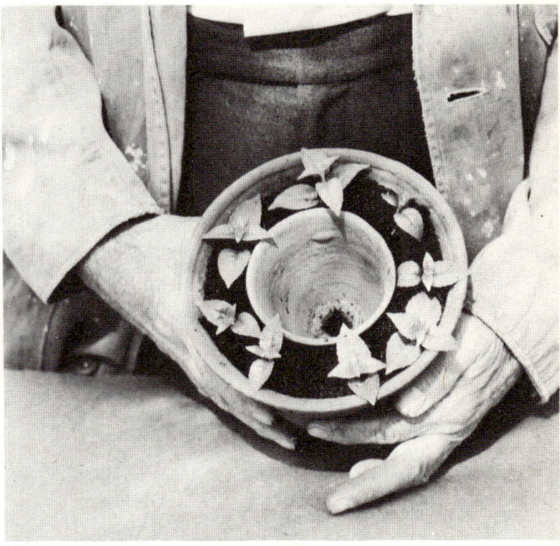

The double-pot shown in the previous picture has now had cuttings inserted. Water is given by pouring it into the small pot and allowing the compost between the two pots to draw up what it needs.

clogging. Firming in a tray is better done with a piece of wood approximately as wide as the tray, but extra attention should be given to the corners of the trays, where compost often lies too loose. Compost which is just moist enough for convenient handling in filling the trays is usually a little dry for sowing. It is customary to partly immerse the tray in a dish of water until the water begins to percolate through to the surface. If the trays are then left overnight to drain, they are ready for sowing next morning. Seed *must* be sown thinly and evenly and then covered with a light dusting of sifted compost. With fine, dust-like seed no such covering is needed. It is enough to press the seed gently with the backs of the fingers to firm it into the surface. The sown box is usually covered with a sheet of glass to retain moisture and a sheet of brown paper to keep out light until the seed germinates. The glass may need watching and wiping dry daily because excess moisture can drip and start such fungus troubles as Damping-Off disease.

However hard you try, it is sometimes impossible to space seed so that pricking out can be avoided. Pricking out means transferring the seedlings to fresh boxes to give them the spacing needed for further development. When pricking out, it is essential to handle the tiny seedlings gently because Damping-Off fungus quickly attacks any bruised soft stems. It is wise to handle the seedlings by their little leaves. Clearly, pricking out is an operation which is worth avoiding, not merely to save work but also to reduce risk of disease. And that is where pelleted seed is a great help to the busy and the inexperienced.

Pelleted seeds are set in a coating which makes them look like little pills. The coating is no guesswork but a mixture evolved during years of research and experiment. It gives the seed not only extra size for easy handling, but protects it from a host of troubles, including pests and diseases which attack naked seed. The coating quickly breaks down in the moist compost, and releases substances to help the seed get a good and sure start. The ease of handling, due to the extra size, gives pelleted seed a great advantage when we come to space the seed during the sowing operation. This means we can place it so as to avoid the need for pricking out.

It is important to remove the glass and paper coverings from the seed-trays when the seed germinates, otherwise the seedlings will be stretched, distorted, and ruined, reaching out for light.

Indoor sowing of items wanted for subsequent outdoor growing have to go through one more critical phase after they have established themselves as sturdy little plants in their seed-trays. They need to be hardened off. This is gardening jargon for weaning them steadily away from the warm conditions of greenhouse or frame to the more exposed conditions of the open garden. Seeds grown in the greenhouse should be given plenty of ventilation, as far as is compatible with watching the interests of other plants in the greenhouse. Then they should be moved to a frame or put under cloches where conditions will be slightly harder but not exposed.

Seedlings started in a frame will need rather less hardening, but in every instance the aim must be to accustom them gradually to less protection until they can manage with none at all. During hardening off, it is usually possible to give fairly exposed conditions by day almost from the start. But covering at night needs to be maintained for rather longer as night conditions are obviously cooler than those of daytime.

One more aid to the busy and inexperienced is to choose F^1 Hybrid seed where such choice exists. F^1 indicates a first-generation cross, which produces a plant

First move in outdoor sowing is to dig the ground

After dug soil has had time to settle it is trodden and thoroughly raked to prepare a fine crumbly surface

A line is stretched and a drill (shallow furrow) for sowing is made with a draw hoe

Seeds are sown thinly and will then be covered and firmed

Seedlings must be thinned out as they grow

Cloches are a good protection and an aid to earlier sowing

having what is termed 'hybrid vigour'. Briefly, this means that it has the combined good qualities of both its parents. This seed is slightly dearer than the general run because the hybridizing which produces it has to be done afresh year after year. The two parent varieties have to be grown (isolated from one another and from all risk of pollination by other plants) and hand-pollination of the female parent has to be done blossom by blossom. Considering all that work, the extra charge is trivial and is more than justified by the high quality and robust health standards of the plants which F^1 seed produces.

17 Friends, Foes, and Chemical Aids

Although there are tens of thousands of insects in your garden – some scientists say *hundreds* of thousands – and most of these insects are pests, there are few you need worry about. You don't need to know a caterpillar from a cutworm (which I will explain later) nor what precise remedy is best for dealing with them. If you can tell a creepy-crawly from a flier, or a sucker from a chewer, you will get by without much trouble. You must have heard of people who at the slightest twinge of pain get out their home guide to medicine. By the time they have read what all the symptoms can mean, they end up convinced that they are suffering from almost every illness in the book. Similarly, there are those who, on learning about any garden pest, can convince themselves that it is doing its mischief in their garden. Which is all nonsense.

Most keen gardeners can quickly learn to recognize a fair range of plant enemies either by sight or by evidence of plant damage. But the gardener for whom we are catering in this book does not need to trouble himself with even that modest amount of detail. It is enough to be able to decide to what group the pest belongs, and there are only three or four groups that matter. That is all I advise busy people to attempt. Providing you do that and stock a handful of remedies plus the right equipment for their easy use, you can write off pests as a trivial problem. There are two extreme views you should guard against. One, which is held by some sincere and intelligent people, is that if you practise something called 'natural methods', nature will keep your garden free of pest damage. The other extreme idea is that you can keep a garden clear of pests by using a powerful kill-all often enough.

The wise aim is to reduce, rather than try to eliminate, plant pests, without killing friendly, predatory insects. These friendly characters kill pests, usually by taking them as food. The trick of being selective, of hitting pests rather than predators, is partly done for us by the scientists who have evolved chemicals which work that way. Another method is timing, by attacking pests while predators' eggs are still unhatched.

One more help to the gardener is the F¹ Hybrid range of plants. These F¹ varieties, with their built-in hybrid vigour, are able to resist pest and disease attacks better than ordinary varieties.

Pests, for the man in a hurry, should be classified simply, rather than identified specifically. As I mentioned earlier, you need not know a caterpillar from a cutworm. But the remedy is much the same. A caterpillar crawls on the plant and eats its leaves. A cutworm chews through the base of the stem so that the plant collapses. What I suggest is that you put the pests into two main categories: the upstairs and the downstairs. Those which work on stems and leaves (upstairs) and those which work on or below the soil surface (downstairs). Without complication we can divide the upstairs workers into two types, suckers and chewers. Then again, we can subdivide the chewers into two shifts, the night-shift and the day-shift. So roughly, it goes like this:

Upstairs (1)	Suckers such as greenfly, blackfly (their lice rather than the flies do the damage), and whitefly.
Upstairs (2)	Chewers (*a*) Day-shift: caterpillars, slugs. (*b*) Night-shift: earwigs, wood-lice, flea beetles, and weevils.
Downstairs	Cutworms, cabbage rootflies, carrot flies, and onion flies. (It is the grubs of these flies that are troublesome.)

My scientist friends will tell me that I have over-simplified, and that some of my night workers and day workers do not always stick to their shifts. We are aware that slugs, for instance, are also around after dark and that there are some aphids which work on roots. But we have to draw lines for simplicity and we are concerned with easy gardening rather than with entomology. Part of the aim must be to guide you on what pests you might expect to see and what you might not see. In daylight, if you shake a plant you might dislodge a snoozing earwig. But that is up to you. Signs you can see, apart from the pests which cause them, are holes in leaves caused by chewers; wrinkling in leaves caused by suckers; broken-down plants where stems have been eaten through; and sickly, droopy plants where soil pests are at work. (A cabbage plant attacked at the roots will become dull and bluish instead of bright green.) Other troubles you may discover will be spotting and discoloration of leaves and stems, sometimes due to physical upsets and sometimes to fungus diseases. Dull white coatings which appear at some seasons are usually easy enough to identify as mildew.

For all these troubles, both pests and diseases, the short-of-time gardener is now finding himself offered easy remedies in the form of what we call 'systemic' chemical controls. These are absorbed into the plant's system and remain effective against pests and diseases which might escape a direct hit at the time of spraying. To show how good these remedies are, let me explain briefly their development. I was privileged to test the first systemic insecticide when it was in its early experimental stage, and I found that a single spraying kept my roses clear of greenfly for the whole season. But the sheer long-lasting quality of the spray made it unacceptable for garden use because if spray had drifted on to food crops it would have made them unsafe to eat.

Scientists have now produced chemical formulations which remain effective long enough to defeat the pest or disease but which break down quickly enough to make them safe to use provided that a few simple rules are followed. Another point is that we can virtually cut out the risk of spray drift if we use a watering-can instead of a fine-nozzle spray, and just water the stuff on to the plants. We know that the leaves and roots will absorb the chemical and let it flow through the plant's sap stream to reach the point where pests or diseases are at work. With fungicides, this abolishes the need to spray every ten to fourteen days in the hope of maintaining a permanent anti-fungus film on leaves and shoots.

Systemic insecticides and systemic fungicides are particularly useful among roses, where greenfly attacks are bad in some years and where Black Spot is a serious fungus trouble. The greenfly referred to is not the fly itself but a nasty little bright green louse. Greenfly have astonishing natures. They can breed without mating and they can produce live young besides eggs. Eggs are laid as winter approaches, but in summer when the female pest is in a hurry, she does not bother egg-laying but reproduces by bearing live young. And she does it at a terrific rate.

The few greenfly missed by sprays which rely on direct hits, could soon have the roses heavily reinfested. But the systemic, working inside the plant, takes care of this risk.

Going back to the easy classification of pests given earlier in this chapter, orthodox remedies, apart from the systemics, are as simple as the classifications. Bromophos will deal with most of the pests which work below soil-level. Slugs are no problem if you use slug pellets. Use them as directed on the packet so as not to risk harm to birds or pets. For above ground, you can get a B.H.C. formulation or old friends like derris and pyrethrum. Pesticide dust can wash off quickly in showery weather, so in such conditions sprays are preferable.

Lawns have their own pest and disease problems which will be dealt with later in this chapter, along with fertilizers and other chemicals, because there are several multi-purpose lawn treatments available nowadays. Greenhouses also call for their own range of chemical aids but these two can be dealt with later when we get around to miscellaneous chemicals.

PLANT NUTRITION

Fertilizers are perhaps the most vital group of plant aids, and yet too many gardeners fail to appreciate the fact. A farmer will probably reckon that every £1 spent on fertilizers makes £10 difference to the value of his crop.

In Chapter 2, we coined the mnemonic PEP, to remind us that Pattern, Equipment, and Plants were basic things to get right, and one of the first things emphasized was the need to feed the ground. If you want to make a test, feed a part of the lawn and leave the rest unfed. You will soon see the difference. To the trained eye, soil hunger is easy to detect. Nine out of every ten gardens that I see are underfed; and there is no excuse except false economy. In the days when people had to spread barrow-load after barrow-load of stable manure, they could have been excused for leaving the soil hungry. But they didn't. Now that it involves no more than scattering the contents of a few bags of plant food, too few do it. Some people spend more in a week on feeding their pets than they spend in a year on feeding the garden. I have seen people take home a 7-lb (3-kg) bag of fertilizer to last the season when it is not enough for a quarter of the average-sized garden. If you fed your budgerigar only one day in four you could not expect him to chatter.

A well-fed garden produces stronger plants, with better resistance to pests, diseases, cold, and drought. If you want an easy garden, feed it well. A simple drill is to use a general fertilizer for most of the garden and give special plant foods to specialist subjects such as lawns and roses. The term 'general' fertilizer indicates one which contains the three main plant foods, nitrogen, potassium, and phosphorus, in quantities so balanced as to create no serious surplus or deficiency in the diet of any plant.

When you buy bags of fertilizer, don't just buy a convenient weight. Work out roughly the ground area to be fed, see how many square yards a bagful will do and buy the size or number of bags required. February and March are good times to apply fertilizers. Lime should be applied at least six weeks before feeding time. Preferably, lime (where needed) should go on in autumn and fertilizer in late winter or spring. In vegetable gardening a popular drill is to divide the plot into three main sections and to lime one of these sections (the one reserved for crops of the cabbage family) each year.

The path weedkiller Pathclear combines paraquat, diquat, and simazine to kill existing weeds and inhibit germination of dormant weed seeds. In this picture the weed-free area is the part where the weedkiller was applied five months previously (in spring). The long-lasting effect is clearly demonstrated.

Plants can be given a booster feed by spraying certain specific nutrients on to the leaves. These can be applied by a pressure-spray or simply poured on through a watering-can fitted with a fine rose. This system is known as 'foliar feeding' and I have heard it called 'systemic feeding'.

There are several brands of liquid fertilizer which can be applied to the soil; and highly concentrated light-weight powders such as Phostrogen. All these are useful for both indoor and certain outdoor feeding. You can also get tablets which are convenient for feeding plants in pots. Phostrogen can be used as a powder or it can be easily dissolved for application as a liquid feed.

WEEDKILLERS

The word 'weedkiller' has taken on a wider meaning and covers a useful gardening technique aimed at controlling growth of unwanted plants with the minimum of effort. General weedkillers, for cleaning pathways and non-cultivated areas, have been with us always. But now we have groups of them for cleaning the ground between plants in cultivation. In one of these groups we have herbicides, whose role is to kill off unwanted growth above ground-level without harming either the roots or upper parts of cultivated plants. Another group aims at suppressing weeds by inhibiting the germination of their seeds lying near the soil surface. Yet another group comprises hormone-type substances which distort weed plants to the point where they can no longer survive. Hormone types (described later) are used on lawns.

Taking first the simplest, the total killer of plant growth, it can be used on paths provided that roots of valuable plants are not at work under the path. I once killed a cherry tree by failing to realize that its roots were reaching out under a path which I was treating with sodium chlorate.

If you use sodium chlorate, get a brand which incorporates a fire suppressant. Neat sodium chlorate is a serious fire hazard. And be careful about names of weedkillers or you can run into awful trouble. One called Weedex is for path weeding and one called Weedol is a herbicide for use among growing plants. It is a pity the names are so similar. If you confuse them and use Weedex in the wrong place, you will have some nasty casualties among your plants. The use of herbicides among plants always calls for care because even when you apply the right chemical, you can do damage by splashing or misdirecting the liquid. The job is made easier by employing the right sort of equipment, which is dealt with in the next chapter.

Lawn weedkillers are a sort of magic, because they are so efficiently selective. You apply them (alone or mixed with nutrients) to the whole lawn and you find that they knock out the weeds while leaving the grass unharmed. The secret is that the structure of the grass leaves (blades) enables them to shed the weedkiller, while the weed leaves cannot shake it off. These killers are based on various hormones, each one being specially suitable for one weed group and only partly successful against other groups. Clover is the most difficult so if you have to kill clover in your lawn be sure to ask your garden chemist for a lawn weedkiller which is prescribed specially for this weed.

Even the friendly domestic cat has to be discouraged at times from scratching among precious plants. First thing to do is to try to provide a spot where dry loose soil is an attraction so that the cat goes there instead of into your plant border. Besides that, you can get various repellents of which the most common is agricultural pepper dust. There are repellents also for spraying on shrubs to discourage birds from taking the berries. These substances, which are harmless, include Morkit, BCD pellets, and Scent-Off Buds.

Ants are not a serious garden pest (though I am not deceived into thinking they are friends) but they are a nuisance when they occupy part of the lawn where you want to sit, or if they march into your pantry. Of the several types of ant control I favour the attractives, such as Panant, which the pests take to their nests and share (fatally) with the whole colony inside. Rooting powders were dealt with in the previous chapter.

Fruit-setting sprays help tomato flowers to set good trusses of fruit without the normal pollination. Bottom trusses on tomato plants frequently fail (except under commercial hot-house conditions) and these sprays are the answer.

Moss-killers are often needed on lawns. Chemicals for dissolving in water are easy to use on mossy patches, and there are lawn treatments combining feeding with the attack on the mosses.

There are some special greenhouse aids, apart from the obvious such as plant foods and routine pesticides and fungicides. Smoke fumigants will drive pest-killer fumes into crevices and other places inaccessible to normal sprays and dusts. Green slime and algae can make pots shabby to look at and unpleasant to handle, but the stuff can be cleaned off with Dimanin. Shading may be needed for the glass in spells of hot sunshine.

A final warning for your *own* protection. Take every precaution advised for handling any chemical. All garden chemicals are safe if the instructions are followed carefully. Almost all can be dangerous if handled stupidly.

18 Give us the Tools

The first part of the garden to equip is the lawn, and the obvious first item for it is the mower. The remarks on mowers here should be read in conjunction with Chapter 6. When you buy a car you can choose according to price, size, performance, comfort, or any factor you like. But when you buy a mower you should choose according to the job you want doing. That concerns not merely what sort or size of lawn you want it to cut, but also what way you want it kept. The casual gardener wants a mower which will keep grass looking reasonably tidy without his having to sweat over it. The simple answer therefore is a rotary mower with an electric motor. Rotary, because that is the type which makes easy work of grass-cutting even in difficult conditions, and electric because there is no problem over starting the engine. But simple answers are not always enough: even a busy man might want a small front lawn looking striped and immaculate. Plenty of people

Systemic insecticides and fungicides do not have to hit the pests or disease spots. They are absorbed by the leaves. If applied as in this picture by simple overhead watering there is no risk of drift on to food crops, as there could be with a fine-mist spray as used for those sprays which kill only by contact with the pest or disease spot.

dislike electricity in the garden and, at the same time, find that petrol-driven engines give them no starting problems. When I say that electric rotary is the easiest I do not mean that others are necessarily difficult. Let us take a brief look at the options. Leave aside for the time being the description of engines, and consider the type of job the machines are designed to do.

Rotary machines, however driven, range from the cutters of long or rough grass, down to those designed for the reasonably fine lawn. Some of them now have seats so that you just sit and steer. One refinement in the rotaries is the hover-type, the Flymo, which has no wheels. The action of its cutter-propeller lifts the machine like a hovercraft so that the skirt just sits on the grass. This virtually eliminates the risk of flying pebbles and the like. Odd items left on the lawn can be flung up dangerously by a wheeled rotary if the cutters are set so high as to leave a big gap under the skirt rim. The two safeguards are to keep the lawn reasonably tidy and to cut it frequently. That way, you need neither have to set the cutters high nor let the grass get long enough to hide nasty little objects. For a steep, grassy slope the hover mower is a boon. Slopes can be slippery and with wheeled machines they are awkward. With the hover mower you can stand firm above the slope, let the machine work down it and then draw it back. You can put a rope on the handle as an extension. There are mini rotaries, electrically operated, which are ideal for the middle-aged and busy housewife with a tiny lawn to keep tidy.

The orthodox type of mower, called a 'cylinder type', has a fixed, bottom blade against which the cylinder of moving blades spins. It is important to check the setting frequently to make sure you are getting a clean cut. With a powered machine, you *must* disconnect the spark-plug or electric lead before making the check. Tip up the machine and check the cutting action on a single blade of grass. If the cutters chew the grass they need adjusting. This involves making just a fraction of a turn of a screw. The reason they need regular checking is that they are usually self-sharpening. This characteristic causes slight wear on the cutters, which needs taking up by adjustment. You can't expect to do easy mowing with a machine that is chewing instead of cutting. However lazy we want to be in our gardening, we must not be so lazy as to neglect machines completely. Minor neglect may involve no more than inconvenience or expense, but you ought to clean and oil your mower, and other garden implements, as soon as you *finish* the job. Soil left on blades dries hard and puts a strain on machine and user. Dampness starts rust which has similar ill effects. Whatever mower you choose, it pays to have a reliable reserve so that a breakdown will not upset you. I have large areas of grass for which I keep rotaries. If you opt for a rotary, you will find that an electric mini rotary is an inexpensive and reliable reserve machine. I use a cylinder type on my show-piece of lawn, and I have a push mower (cylinder type) as a stand-by.

When you are choosing engines, here are points to consider. An electric motor starts at the flick of a switch and nothing could be easier. If it is powered direct from the mains, and the flex is a problem, you can get an extension coil to set up a temporary power-point right where you need it. This extension is useful for all tools powered by mains-electric motors. If you do not like electric flex in the garden, you can get a battery-electric motor, complete with charger. Four-stroke petrol engines are popular, but a two-stroke engine is better for some jobs. Without being too technical, I had better explain why. The four-stroke engine is lubricated by a reservoir of oil which splashes round the moving parts of the engine. A two-stroke engine runs on a mixture of petrol and lubricating oil (instead of neat petrol) so needs no separate oil reservoir. The lubrication system in a four-stroke engine works most efficiently when the engine is on the level. If it is tilted to operate on a steep slope, the oil can fail to circulate properly and the engine can suffer damage. This disadvantage does not apply to the lubrication system of the two-stroke engine. Whichever of these engines you use, you might like to follow my practice of turning off the fuel a few seconds before finishing the job, so that the carburettor can run dry. If there is no 'on-off' fuel-tap there is probably a vent screw in the filler-cap. When you screw this down, the petrol flow stops because of lack of air. If you have this sort of filler-cap, don't forget to reopen the vent before you try to use the engine again. Not everyone makes a regular habit of emptying the carburettor as I do, but after years of the practice I am sure it works; stagnant petrol is liable to form a gooey sediment.

If you never use a grass-box the lawn can become slightly matted or choked on the surface. The hard way to cope with this is a thorough raking, such as keen lawnsmen do annually. But the easy way, when necessary, is to use a powered rake or scarifier. This looks like a sort of cross between a motor mower and a mechanical cultivator. Dealers have it available for hire. You don't need to own one.

A wheeled spreader takes the labour out of feeding the lawn. And when necessary, you can use it for a combined weeder-feeder or mosskiller-feeder to do two jobs in one.

For applying liquid weedkiller or mosskiller over a whole lawn, the quick aid is a watering-can fitted with a T-shaped, perforated bar instead of the usual rose-end. This allows you to work accurately in strips. If you have odd patches to treat on an otherwise clean lawn, use a bucket and hand-brush. Just slosh the appropriate liquid on to the weedy patches by flicking the brush after dipping it in the bucket.

The only other labour-saving lawn tool I want to mention is the powered edger. You steer it round the edges to make them sharp and neat. I prefer to avoid even that bit of easy labour where possible by letting the lawn edges merge into hedges or into plants hanging over the edge between border and grass.

The electric hedge-trimmer is a big help to anyone who has to keep a hedge tidy. Study the instructions, and work away from the flex (if mains-powered) so that you do not cut into it. You can get an electric trimmer which is worked by a small, rechargeable battery.

Every garden needs a hose at times. I keep mine on a reel which is fixed to the wall. Water feeds the hose through the reel, from a stand-pipe. This takes the struggle out of hose-handling. One just carries the hose-end to where it is wanted, and winds it back on to the reel afterwards.

A roller is not a necessity. I have one which is weighted by being filled with water, but I use it mostly for firming gravel into paths. An annual rolling might help a lawn which is mown always by a non-roller mower. But remember that a roller is not intended to flatten down bumps. These should be levelled by spadework. The roller's job is to consolidate roots by a gentle firming, and the light roller incorporated in mowers is heavy enough.

A wheelbarrow should be strong but not heavy or unbalanced. Mine has a metal frame with a strong plastic body.

There is a plastic container with non-spill cap and assorted dribble-bars made specially for applying the weedkiller Weedol on weeds close up to plants without

This specially designed can enables a herbicide, such as Weedol, to be applied to weeds growing right up to the plant. There is no splashing or spilling to injure the plant.

A sprayer which incorporates its own pump. Pumping puts the liquid under pressure and the operator then has both hands free for spraying. The spray-lance has an adjustable nozzle.

This type of plastic-hose connection is available in a wide range of fittings for coupling hoses to taps or to items of equipment such as sprinklers, and also for joining together lengths of hose. The action is a simple snap-on and snap-off.

fear of splashing. Dribble-bars are thin tubes with tiny perforations so that they allow accurate distribution along a strip as narrow as 3 inches (7 cm), or wider when required.

The easiest type of sprayer has a built-in air-pump. One can pump up a high pressure which will push out the spray as a fine jet. It makes work light, because the pumping and spraying, which are both easy, are two separate operations. The nozzle is usually adjustable and easy to clear if a spot of grit gets in. For spot-spraying, get insecticides in aerosol packs.

If you have a greenhouse, hang a maximum-and-minimum thermometer inside. Outside, have a frost predictor (strangely called a 'wet and dry bulb thermometer'). The max-min thermometer has metal markers which stay at the high and low readings until you reset them with a magnet. They tell you just how low the temperature fell in the coldest part of the night and how high it went in the hottest part of the day.

The general run of hand tools and minor equipment is still to be considered, and it is wise to choose carefully. Buy brand-names you know to be good, or buy from a firm which has a reputation to keep up. Assuming you follow this advice, there is no need to go into detail about each item. Nor need you buy every item in the following list. You certainly need not buy all at once. But get them when the need is recognized.

Spade. This is a much-maligned tool. Used properly it is an effortless piece of equipment. Stand close up to it. Take thin and small slices of soil on it, and never bend forward with a loaded spade in your hand. Check for balance. That means holding it as you might in digging and seeing that it does not feel heavy-ended.

Garden Fork. Much the same applies here as to the spade. The fork can help you break up soil easily when full spadework is not needed.

Border Spade and Fork. These two tools are smaller versions of the other two. Apart from their original use among plants in an established border, they are popular with women, who find them lighter in use.

Rakes. First is the garden rake, which has stiff fingers (call them tines or teeth) for crumbling the soil with a pull-and-push action, especially where you aim to sow seed. Second is the lawn rake, the conventional type of which has springy tines so that they do not dig in and tear up the lawn. It loosens and pulls out dead and matted grass growth.

Hoes. There are two kinds of these too. The Dutch hoe has a blade set at only a slight angle from the shaft. It is used to cut down weeds by a sliding action at or barely below the surface, and also to loosen caking soil. The draw hoe has a deeper blade, set at near right angles to the shaft. One of its uses, when tilted so that only a corner contacts the soil, is to draw little furrows (drills) for seed to be sown in.

Hand Fork and Trowel. These two tools do on a very small scale some of the jobs done by the spade and garden fork. There is plenty of work for the trowel when small plants are being set out, and the fork is convenient for easing out weed roots close to plants which do not want to be disturbed.

Garden Shears. Everyone knows this tool which is in popular use for such jobs as trimming privet hedges. Until you get your electric hedge-trimmer you can use these shears. And afterwards they will be a useful stand-by.

Pruning Shears. This tool is simply a pair of efficient snippers. Even if you do little or no recognized pruning, you will find much use for such shears when you want to cut a few flowers or trim an awkward shoot which is getting in your way.

Edging Shears. These are similar in action to garden shears, except that they have long handles, set at a different angle so that you can trim lawn edges without any awkward bending.

Sprinkler. This is another lawn item, but may have uses elsewhere in the garden in dry weather. Attach it to a hose, turn on the water, and the force of water spins the sprinkler to send out a circular fine shower.

Snap-on hose fittings. These plastic connectors ease the work of coupling hose to tap and to other equipment.

If your garage lacks the spare capacity to house your garden tools and machines, work out all your needs before you decide what size of garden shed to buy. And be sure its door is wide enough.

One final time-saver of mine is to paint the handles of all garden tools a vivid orange-scarlet. When I forget where I have left them, it does not take me long to find them, even in the grass.

Index

Illustrations indicated by *italic numerals*

CARTERS
DICTIONARY OF GARDENING

Compiled by Oliver Dawson

A lavishly illustrated garden dictionary, covering not only flowers, trees, and vegetables, but also general gardening techniques. It has been compiled for Carters by the author of six popular books and many articles on all aspects of gardening, and will appeal equally to professional gardeners and to enthusiastic amateurs. Most of the beautiful illustrations have been drawn by Leslie Greenwood.

256 pp. 260 × 190 cm/192 colour illustrations/SBN 434 90298 5

CARTERS
BOOK FOR GARDENERS

A. G. L. Hellyer
M.B.E., F.L.S., V.M.H., A.H.R.H.S.

Published in collaboration with Carters Tested Seeds Ltd, here is a book of universal appeal. Beginners, as well as the more experienced; those with small, medium or large gardens; people who enjoy growing house plants; in fact, all who garden as a hobby will gain a great deal from this wise and practical book.

The author, who has a string of best-sellers to his name, presents simply but thoroughly all the facts the gardener needs in dealing with:

Planning
Lawns and pavings
Screens and hedges
Annuals and bedding plants
Bulbs, corms, and tubers
Hardy plants
Roses
Shrubs and climbers
Trees
Rock and water features
Greenhouse and frame
Vegetables
Herb beds
Fruit
Feeding plants
Keeping plants healthy
Weed control

Extensive colour illustrations enhance the text in every chapter, many of which have also quick-reference tables to guide the reader in successfully growing a great range of plants, shrubs, and trees.

Practical work in the garden is made clear with a series of drawings specially commissioned from Mike Taylor, all in full colour. Dimensions are given in metric units as well as the more familiar English ones so that the text is intelligible to the widest audience here and abroad.

A. G. L. Hellyer. It is no exaggeration to describe Arthur Hellyer as the doyen of writers on gardening. In addition to being the author of numerous books, he has edited *Amateur Gardening* (1946–67), *Gardening Illustrated* (1947–56), and he is the gardening correspondent of *The Financial Times*. He writes from extensive practical experience, being the owner of two gardens himself: one on heavy land in a frost pocket in Sussex and the other in a dry, sunny quarry in Jersey.

160 pp. 235 × 155 cm/186 colour photographs/104 line drawings/tables/index/SBN 434 90725 1